THE BATTLE OF
MATAPAN
1941

'The Mediterranean is an absurdly small sea; the length and greatness of
its history makes us dream it larger than it is.'
Lawrence Durrell, *The Alexandria Quartet: Balthazar*

For the members of my family past and present who have served in the
Royal Navy and Royal Marines.

MARK SIMMONS

THE BATTLE OF MATAPAN 1941

THE TRAFALGAR OF THE MEDITERRANEAN

SPELLMOUNT

Front cover: 'Warspite Recovers her Swordfish.' HMS *Warspite* picks up her reconnaissance plane at speed, a manoeuvre never tried out before as the British Fleet steam flat out to catch the Italian warships. The Swordfish piloted by Petty Officer Ben Rice had been aloft for nearly five hours, searching in vain for the Italian fleet. Low on fuel the aircraft was recovered by the fast moving *Warspite* in a challenging operation that was faultlessly accomplished. (Painting by Dennis C. Andrews)

Mark Simmons served in the Royal Marines in the 1970s. He is now a full-time writer specialising in military history and is the author of two novels, *From the Foam of the Sea* and *The Serpent and the Cross.*

First published 2011 by Spellmount, an imprint of
The History Press
The Mill, Brimscombe Port
Stroud, Gloucestershire, GL5 2QG
www.thehistorypress.co.uk

Maps on pages 10, 39, 101 and 123 by Martin Brown Design
© The History Press

British Library Cataloguing in Publication Data.
A catalogue record for this book is available from the British Library.

ISBN 978 0 7524 5829 8

Typesetting and origination by The History Press
Printed in Great Britain

Contents

	Acknowledgements	7
	Prologue	9
	Introduction	11
Part 1	The Naval War in the Mediterranean, June 1940–March 1941	
1	The Fourth Punic War	15
2	The Regia Marina	19
3	Britain Alone	23
4	Ultra Secret	29
5	Early Clashes	33
6	Operation Judgement	45
7	Cape Spartivento	57
8	Enter the Luftwaffe	63
Part 2	Matapan	
9	Reluctant Allies	75
10	Hut 8	83
11	The British Fleet at Alexandria	87
12	Daybreak, 28 March	93
13	Morning, 28 March	97
14	Afternoon, 28 March	103
15	Attack at Dusk	113
16	Night Action 28/29 March	119

17   The Italian Cruisers   129
18   29 March   135

Part 3 Conclusions

19   Effects of Matapan   141
20   Intelligence   151
21   What If   155

Appendix A The British Fleet at Matapan   169
Appendix B The Italian Fleet at Matapan   175
Appendix C The Aircraft at Matapan   181

        Bibliography   183
        Index   187

Acknowledgements

The genesis of this book came about while researching some articles on the Taranto Raid. It struck me there were some relatively recent books on the Taranto Raid but not on Matapan. I am grateful to the veterans of the Second World War whom I spoke to, and through whom it was made apparent to me that the battle, particularly in three key areas, needed exploring again. This was not to detract from the older excellent accounts of the Battle of Matapan, S.W.C. Pack's *The Battle of Matapan* which is largely an eyewitness account by the weatherman of HMS *Formidable* which I have quoted several times, and Ronald Seth's *Two Fleets Surprised: The Battle of Cape Matapan*, which is different in its approach, exploring the Italian side of events more fully. Both are now 50 years old and much new material pertaining to the battle has become available since their publication. Neither of the earlier versions make any reference to the Ultra decodes, the name used by British intelligence resulting from the decryption of encrypted Axis radio communications in the Second World War. They could not have mentioned the vital part Bletchley Park played in the battle, as the information was not declassified until the mid 1970s.

I am hugely indebted to Group Captain L.E. (Robbie) Robins AEDL, who drew my attention to much of the role Ultra played, and gave me free use of his extensive library, supplied numerous cups of coffee and great conversation and was good enough to read an early draft making many excellent comments and suggestions. And to David Pearce my architect, another avid book collector who introduced me to Robbie, which proved such a great favour.

The second area was to reassess the Italian side of events. Count Galeazzo Ciano's diary gave a flavour of Italian High Command political and military at the highest levels. Commander Marc Antonio Bragadin's *The Italian Navy in World War II* has been invaluable, as has the help of C.V. Francesco at the Italian Navy Historical Archives.

Thirdly the role of Admiral of the Fleet Lord Cunningham of Hyndhope as C-in-C Mediterranean Fleet in 1941 needed some assessment, as his role has become rather tarnished in recent years. Cunningham's own autobiography *A Sailor's Odyssey* was a vital source. The HMSO official British histories have also been a gold mine of information.

Many associations have helped with eyewitness accounts and illustrations. Ray Oliver and Sara Wrigley at the HMS *Barham* association, Russ Graystone at the HMAS *Perth* association, Denis W. Edwards at the HMS *Formidable* association and Frank Allen at the HMS *Hood* association. Also the BBC's WW2 People's War archive, for the memories of Surgeon-Commander E.R. Sorley RN supplied by Graeme Sorley.

I also want to thank many museums for their help with illustrations. In particular the Royal Navy Museum Portsmouth, Fleet Air Arm Museum Yeovilton, the Italian Navy Historical Archives, the Venice Naval History Museum, the Imperial War Museum and the United States Navy Historical Centre.

Iain Ballantyne and Dennis C. Andrews (who also provided the artwork for the front cover) at *International Fleet Review*, John Mussell at *Medal News* and Flint Whitlock at *World War II* magazines gave me much encouragement, advice and help.

My Wife Margaret as always gave her wholehearted support in proofreading and index building with additional help from Jo Shinner. My Father A.F.T (Tom) Simmons ran his expert sailor's eye over the manuscript and assisted with illustrations. Thanks to all.

Prologue

'Here we are safely back in harbour after taking part in what has been rightly described as "the greatest naval battle of the war".' So wrote Surgeon-Commander E.R. Sorley in April 1941, who served on the battleship *Barham*, part of the golden generation that fought during the Second World War, sadly fast disappearing now. He tried to analyse the Battle of Matapan: 'Our success was due to (a) an extraordinary piece of good fortune in coming close enough to the enemy in the dark (b) the Italians' ignorance of our whereabouts and (c) our very prompt seizing of the opportunity before the enemy could escape.'[1]

Of course Sorley could not have known there was rather more to it than that; vital aspects responsible for victory were hidden. The Italian fleet was hamstrung by its own countrymen and allies. A labyrinth of Axis politics and strategies did it no favours. Yet it might have turned out differently had another course been taken.

And then there are the voices of those who took part from admirals, to pilots and the ratings of the lower decks; all were heroes in the long story of men at sea.

Note
1   BBC World War II archives. Surgeon-Commander E.R. Sorley

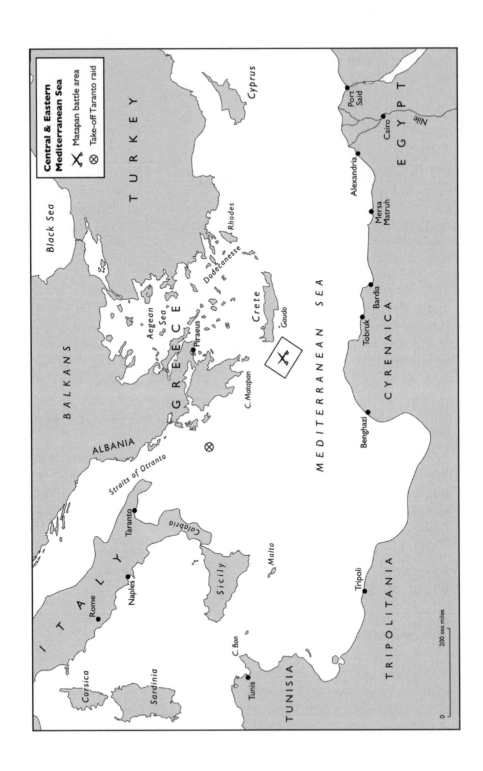

Central & Eastern Mediterranean Sea

✗   Matapan battle area

⊗   Take-off Taranto raid

Black Sea

TURKEY

Cyprus

Port
Said

Cairo

Nile

EGYPT

Alexandria

Mersa
Matruh

Rhodes

Dodecanesse

BALKANS

Aegean
Sea

G R E E C E

Piraeus

Crete

Ġaudo

C. Matapan

Bardia

Tobruk

CYRENAICA

ALBANIA

Straits of Otranto

M E D I T E R R A N E A N   S E A

Benghazi

Taranto

Calabria

Naples

Rome

I T A L Y

Sicily

Malta

Tripoli

TRIPOLITANIA

Corsica

Sardinia

C. Bon

Tunis

TUNISIA

0   200 sea miles

Introduction

It was the humid season on Malta, that September of 1943. The hot Sirocco winds from North Africa blow from August to October across the cool sea, raising humidity. The local sailors do not like them because the seas have time to build up and on land they can bring bad dust storms to the Maltese islands and Sicily. However, the weather was clear on the day the Italian fleet came to surrender.

On 10 September 1943, a haze reduced visibility to some fifteen miles. *Warspite* and *Valiant*, two British veteran battleships of Matapan, with escorting destroyers, went out to meet the Italian vessels. Both battleships had been present 25 years before, with the 5th Battle Squadron, when in November 1918 the German High Seas Fleet had surrendered at the end of the First World War. They had met the Italians off the coast of Africa, north of Bone, the Italian ships sailing from Spezia early on 9 September. The latter had taken an agreed course west of Corsica, a fleet of three battleships, six cruisers and eight destroyers. The three battleships of the *Vittorio Veneto* class were the newest in the fleet; *Roma* had only been completed in 1942.

The Italian ships were attacked by dozens of German aircraft from bases in the south of France, using the new FX-1400 'Fitz X' guided bombs, in the gulf of Asinara near Sardinia. *Roma* was hit on the port side; speed was quickly reduced to ten knots. Another bomb hit between the bridge and second 15-inch gun turret resulting in a magazine explosion. The ship burst into flames and quickly capsized and sank, taking 1,350 men down with her. The *Littorio* (renamed the *Italia* after the fall of Mussolini) was slightly damaged. Other Italian naval units sailed to Malta from several ports. In all 5 battleships, 8 cruisers, 7 destroyers, 24 torpedo-boats, 40 submarines, 19 corvettes and various auxiliaries and smaller vessels surrendered.

Admiral Andrew Browne Cunningham, commander of the British Mediterranean Fleet, known affectionately as ABC, was delighted. 'It was the most moving and thrilling sight. To see my wildest hopes of years back brought to fruition.'[1] The most deadly enemy to Britain's control of the Mediterranean had been brought to heel, directly the result of the victories of Taranto and Matapan.

Modern Italy almost from its first unification had cast covetous eyes toward Malta. In 1866 she had entered an alliance with Prussia against Austria but had come off worst both on land and sea. The result was the navy was rebuilt with the most powerful ships, the *Duilio* class battleships with four 100-ton Armstrong guns mounted in pairs in revolving turrets, their design directly influenced by the USS *Monitor* of the American Civil War.

Britain could not risk any likely threat to its route through the Mediterranean Sea to its imperial territories. Although no state of war existed between the two countries, Malta and Gibraltar were vital coaling stations. The answer, the deterrent, was to build four great coastal batteries armed with the same 100-ton guns, all built by Armstrong's of Newcastle, one of which can still be seen at the Rinella Gun Battery on Malta. During the Second World War it became a coast watching post for the 2nd Battalion Cheshire Regiment, whilst its rock-hewn galleries became air raid shelters.[2] Therefore it was a great achievement that on 11 September 1943 Cunningham was able to send a signal to the Admiralty; 'Be pleased to inform their Lordships that the Italian Battle Fleet now lies at anchor under the guns of the fortress of Malta.'[3]

The people of the island rejoiced as the Italians surrendered. 'Malta was en fete, with the people wild with jubilation and many of the streets draped in flags. Among others, the parish priest of shattered Senglea contiguous to the dockyard and therefore one of the main targets of air attack announced the Italian surrender from his pulpit.'[4] The outlook in June 1940 could hardly have been more different. The day after Italy's declaration of war on Britain and France, the air raids hit Malta, bombs falling on Pieta, Floriana, and lower Valetta.

Notes
1 Cunningham, A.B. *A Sailor's Odyssey* p.563
2 Farrugia, Mario, *Fort Rinella* p.33
3 Cunningham, p.564
4 Ibid p.565

PART 1

The Naval War in the Mediterranean, June 1940–March 1941

1

The Fourth Punic War

Late in the afternoon of 10 June 1940 Benito Mussolini, *Il Duce*, spoke from the balcony of the Palazzo Venezia in Rome to the crowd which had been hurriedly assembled. An order approving the demonstration had only been signed the day before, so the faithful could share the moment.

'Destiny' *Il Duce* proclaimed, had decreed war. 'We go into the field against the plutocratic and reactionary democracies' who had 'threatened the existence of the Italian people.' The speech was delivered in his usual bellicose style; 'Honour, self-interest and the future' could not be ignored. He declared Italy's naval intentions: 'We want to snap the territorial and military chains which suffocate us in our sea ... [Italy] cannot really be free if it does not have free access to the ocean.'[1]

Mussolini was speaking to the ranks of his ardent fascist supporters. The view of many other Italians was rather different. Public opinion in September 1939 had rejoiced at the decision to remain neutral. In the intervening months it had not changed. Even among *Il Duce*'s closest supporters and advisors, support for the Pact of Steel with Germany and entry into the war was lukewarm, or people were openly hostile. Count Galeazzo Ciano, his son-in-law and Minister of Foreign Affairs, son of Costanzo Ciano, the admiral, war hero and ardent fascist supporter, was against the alliance. In his celebrated diary Ciano leaves a picture of his struggle to restrain his father-in-law in his support for Hitler and the Nazis. He warned him the war would be long, arduous and would be won by the British.[2] On the day Mussolini made the announcement, Ciano wrote in his diary: 'The news of war does not surprise anyone and does not cause very much enthusiasm. I am sad, very sad. The adventure begins. May God help Italy.'[3] The Italian General Staff convened at the Palazzo Venezia a few days earlier and had warned Mussolini that Italy was ill-prepared, and the war must be short. 'Our supplies are frighteningly low. We literally don't have some metals. On the eve of the war – and what a war – we have only 100 tons of nickel.'[4]

Italy had been living on a war basis since 1935. Her adverse trading balance was large and the government's budget for 1939–40 forecast a heavy deficit. A further arms race could be disastrous. The Italian Army was undergoing a major reorganisation, involving the reduction of infantry divisions from three regiments to two; the process was ongoing, and a serious handicap to large operations. Between January and April a big call up of conscripts and reservists had taken place. The army had some recent experience of campaigning but not against a modern enemy, and there were shortages of weapons and equipment, and much they had was outdated.

The *Regia Aeronautica* (Italian Air Force) had some 5,400 aircraft, but 400 were obsolete and based in the African colonies, and the Service had reached a peak of readiness for war in 1936. Since then a decline had set in. It was only fit to fight a short modern war. In contrast the morale of the *Regia Marina* (Italian Navy), a problem from its creation, had improved under the fascist regime. It had good ships: well built, well armed and fast. However it lacked a secure supply of oil and lacked experience, and had carried out too few exercises to bring the ships up to full efficiency. The submarine fleet by its size alone deserved respect; in 1940 it had twice as many boats as the Kreigsmarine.[5] According to reports from the Italian Commission for War Production, which reached Mussolini at the end of 1939, Italian industry would begin to meet in full the needs of the three armed forces by 1944. By February 1940 General Favagrossa, head of the commission, was able to report that the former date could be brought forward to 1943.

Mussolini was gambling that the war would be short, although however short it might be, Italy would be dependent for raw materials on her German ally, although *Il Duce* was determined to fight his own war at British and French expense.[6] According to the *New York Times*:

With the courage of a jackal at the heels of a bolder beast of prey, Mussolini had now left his ambush. His motives in taking Italy into the war are as clear as day. He wants to share in the spoils which he believes will fall to Hitler, and he has chosen to enter the war when he thinks he can accomplish this at the least cost to himself.[7]

Winston Churchill said that the responsibility for Italy entering the war was borne by 'one man alone'; certainly many Italians were unenthusiastic. For Mussolini, victory was less important than fighting itself, for it was 'humiliating to remain with our hands folded while others write history. It matters little who wins.'[8] By 1940 he had been in power for eighteen years; in the early days many had admired him and his policies. Clementine Churchill who met him in 1926 thought him 'One of the most wonderful men of our times.' She was delighted to take away a signed photo as a memento, which she kept on her desk for some time.[9] Winston Churchill himself, in a 1927 speech in Rome, declared that Mussolini's fascist movement had 'rendered a service to the entire world', with its stand against 'the bestial appetites and passions of Leninism.'[10]

Many Italians, although they mistrusted Hitler, felt they were opportunistically entering a short war for profit. France was on her knees, the BEF had lost all its heavy equipment and had barely escaped Dunkirk, and some of her leaders talked of abandoning the Mediterranean. In June 1940 Mussolini's gamble hardly seemed risky, and few demurred openly at his decision. The alliance with Germany would free Italy to pursue her own agenda in the Mediterranean and Africa. Mussolini expressed this three years later to party officials. 'The question of our land frontiers was settled by the war of 1915–18. We are faced today with the problem of maritime frontiers, and this conflict has for us a very special character, that of the Fourth Punic War.'[11] The Italian fleet would play a central role in this.

> To make a people great it is necessary to send them to battle even if you have to kick them in the ass. This is what I shall do. I do not forget that in 1918 there were 540,000 deserters in Italy. And if we do not take advantage of this opportunity to pit our navy against the French and British forces, what is the use of building 600,000 tons of warships? Some coast guards and some yachts would be enough to take the young ladies on a joy ride.[12]

Notes

1 Bosworth, R.J.B. *Mussolini* p.369
2 Ciano, G. *Ciano's Diary 1937–1943* p.341, 347
3 Ibid p.362
4 Ibid p.357
5 Playfair, Major-General I.S.O. *The Mediterranean and Middle East Volume 1* p.39
6 Deakin, F.W. *The Brutal Friendship* p.12
7 *New York Times* 11 June 1940
8 Bosworth, p.369
9 Ibid p.370
10 Garibaldi, Luciano, *Mussolini: The Secrets of his Death* p.130
11 Deakin, p.6
12 Ciano, p.341

2

The Regia Marina

When Italy declared war in June 1940 the armed forces had been on a war footing since the Ethiopian campaign of 1935. For a brief period after that some Regia Marina (Italian Navy) auxiliary services were reduced but by the end of 1936 the Spanish Civil War broke out in which Italy became heavily involved. That was followed by various international crises, and finally the occupation of Albania in April 1939.

The Regia Marina had planned – like the other services – for a major war in 1942; when war came in 1940 it was far from ready. It had only two of the *Andrea-Doria* class of reconstructed battleships in commission; built during the First World War, they had been completely modernised, weighing 23,622 tons and with a speed of 27 knots they mounted 10 12.6-inch guns, 12 5.2-inch, 10 3.5-inch and 19 37mm anti-aircraft guns. Armour protection had also been improved over the magazines and vital machinery areas. A main armament gun turret had been removed from the midship section to reduce weight. Two more ships of the class, *Duilio* and *Doria*, were near to entering service after a similar reconstruction.[1]

More impressive were the *Vittorio Veneto* class (also known as *Littorio* class) ships; four vessels were laid down making use of the maximum dimensions permitted by the Washington naval treaty. They displaced 35,000 tons and were capable of 30 knots. They mounted 9 15-inch guns and 12 6-inch, 4 4.7-inch, 12 3.5-inch and some 50 anti-aircraft guns.[2] These ships were comparable to the British *King George V* class battleships. However they were more heavily armed and armoured and faster than the British *Queen Elizabeth* class predominately used by the Royal Navy in the Mediterranean. Work on the fourth ship of the class *Impero* was ultimately suspended in 1943; *Roma* (the third) did enter service in the spring of 1943.

Two more years might have helped the Regia Marina to improve any technical weakness in its vessels, but it was also behind most of the other leading navies in the areas of night fighting, torpedo launching, radar and asdic. Lack of radar in particular hampered early warning, gunnery, and night actions. Radar and asdic were well known in principle, but home industries were well behind in research and development. It was only towards the end of the war that the navy received a few experimental radar sets.[3]

In most areas of supply the navy was well catered for. The naval shipyards worked throughout the war, using almost exclusively supplies stockpiled before the conflict. Changing fortunes in the Libyan desert war forced the navy to re-equip various ports several times from its own stocks. At times it even helped out the other armed services as well.

However in the supply of fuel oil the navy was always hampered. In June 1940 the navy had 1,800,000 tons of oil stored. Under war conditions it was estimated the fleet would need 200,000 tons per month. However Mussolini considered this more than enough for the 'three month campaign', which he felt was the likely duration of the war. He even insisted the navy give up 300,000 tons to the Regia Aeronautica (Italian Air Force) and civilian industry. As the war progressed the Regia Marina was gradually forced to limit ship movements to reduce consumption. By 1943 it was down to 24,000 tons a month.

Commander Marc Antonio Bragadin wrote: 'Following its service tradition the navy was largely impervious to Fascist political infiltration.' This was true up to a point and certainly true of the older aristocratic officers, but many of the younger officers had been imbued with Fascist principles.[4] Admiral Cunningham visited the Italian Naval Academy at Livorno (Leghorn) in 1934, and observed

the Italians appeared to give their young officers a good training which ended in an extensive cruise on a sailing training ship. According to our values the discipline was unnecessarily harsh, imprisonment in a cell being awarded for quite minor offences. The Italian Navy was always royalist, and such conversations as I had with the more senior officers disclosed considerable resentment with the Fascist Regime, particularly because two Fascist officials, in the guise of physical training experts, had recently been appointed to the staff presumably to keep an eye on what went on and to indoctrinate the cadets in the Fascist creed.[5]

Although Benito Mussolini had been Prime Minister and was dictator of Italy, unlike Adolf Hitler he never became head of state. His Black Shirts might swear loyalty to him but the armed forces did not. Their allegiance was to King Victor Emmanuel III, and it was the power of the King through the armed forces that removed Mussolini from power in 1943.[6]

In 1938 Cunningham was entertained to lunch on board the battle-ship *Conte di Cavour* when an Italian squadron visited Malta. He found the battleships 'fine examples of old ships modernised and the work had been skilfully done.' He came to the conclusion such was their reception, 'that he [Admiral Riccardi] must have embarked the whole catering staff and band from one of the best hotels in Rome, so distinguished was his entertainment.' He found he 'liked Admiral Riccardi and the senior officers who were most courteous and pleasant. The younger officers however, were ill-mannered and boorish.'[7]

On the whole before the war the two navies had a good relationship. For the Regia Marina it was a pity a good relationship did not exist with the air force, the Regia Aeronautica. The four major navies of the world in the years after the First World War had come to the conclusion individually that it was critical to develop aircraft carriers and a naval air arm. The Regia Marina did develop its own air arm at this time, but with the creation of the Regia Aeronautica in 1923 the navy was ordered to discontinue all aviation activity.

In Britain towards the end of the First World War, when the Royal Air Force came into being, the Royal Navy also had to hand over all its air-craft and personnel. The RAF then controlled naval aviation for the next 21 years. However the relationship between the two services, although prickly at times, did bear fruit. Naval aviation made significant progress, and just in time for the Second World War an independent Fleet Air Arm was formed.

In Italy Mussolini and the Regia Aeronautica argued that the Italian peninsula represented a great aircraft carrier in the middle of the Mediterranean. Therefore naval proposals to build carriers were firmly rejected. Had the two services worked in close tandem this might have been a reasonable stance. However the Regia Aeronautica greatly overrated its own capabilities. Count Ciano observed: 'The usual air force boasts were inspired by their hatred and distrust of the navy.'[8] An example of this hubris was that the air force entered the war with no torpedo-carrying aircraft and only developed one, with naval help, once the war was in full swing.[9] During the war the two Italian services made great efforts to overcome their difficulties but years of neglect and mistrust could not be quickly forgotten. The result was that the navy fought its war without adequate air cover, and more specifically a lack of aircraft carriers. In 1941 Mussolini realised his mistake and directed that two big ocean liners under construction be converted to aircraft carriers. The liner *Roma,* renamed the *Aquila,* and the liner *Augustus,* which became the *Sparviero* were taken over. All too late however, as both ships never entered service. By 1943 *Aquila* was finished, only waiting for its aircraft.[10]

On the whole the Supermarina, the Italian Navy High Command was a top-heavy, overly hierarchical organisation. Practically its 'operations rooms' worked well, although failed to develop ideas and strategy. Only through its smaller units did the navy display a genius for ideas which had little import from the high command. Admiral Wilhelm Canaris, head of the Abwehr (German Intelligence Service), said to Field Marshal Erwin Rommel:

> The Italian Navy has for the most part excellent qualities, which should enable it to stand up to the best navies in the world. It is too bad that its High Command lacks decision. But this probably is because it has to work under the disordered directives of the Italian Supreme Command which is controlled by the Army.[11]

Notes
1 Preston, Antony, *Jane's Fighting Ships of World War II* p.162
2 Ibid p.163
3 Bragadin, M.A. *The Italian Navy in World War II* p.4
4 Ibid p.5
5 Cunningham, A.B. *A Sailor's Odyssey* p.162–163
6 Bosworth, R.J.B. *Mussolini* p.401
7 Cunningham, p.190–191
8 de Belat, R. *The Struggle for the Mediterranean 1939–1945* p.68
9 Bragadin, p.11
10 Ibid p.98–99
11 Ibid p.13

3

Britain Alone

On 22 June 1940, the aged Marshal Petain, as head of the French Government, signed an armistice with Germany. Britain was alone. But this was not to say that the inhabitants of the island were truly alone, as Britain had the considerable support of her Empire. From Canada, Australia, New Zealand and India, troops flooded into Britain, although it took the collapse of the coalition government in South Africa under Barry Hertzog before that country declared war, under a new administration formed by Jan Smuts. Foreign cruisers and destroyers joined the Royal Navy and later the 8th Army would be made up with units from all corners of the Empire.

With the threat of a cross-channel invasion looming and Italy's entry into the war, the First Sea Lord, Admiral Sir Dudley Pound, suggested on 17 June that the Mediterranean Fleet should sail for Gibraltar, where it could better support the Home Fleet and the vital trade routes across the Atlantic, thus withdrawing from the eastern Mediterranean. Admiral Cunningham 'replied later the same day, detailing my proposed arrangements for the withdrawal of the navy, saying that the possibility had already been considered by General Wavell, and that in this event it was his opinion that Egypt could not be held for long.'[1] On paper this was not an unreasonable stance for the Admiralty to take. The number of Italian troops in Libya so greatly outnumbered the British Army of the Nile that the safe retention of Alexandria as a supply base was in question. However Winston Churchill would have none of it. The Mediterranean must be held; anything less would be tantamount to giving up the Empire. And from the Mediterranean, Jews, Arabs, Maltese and Cypriots had flocked to the colours.

Egypt itself had been in the throes of a major political crisis; Mohammad Mahmoud Pasha had resigned and had been replaced by the chief of the royal household, Aly Maher Pasha. This was an indication that the government, perhaps, did not reflect the anti-German feeling of the people. Egypt would become a hotbed of clandestine Axis-Fascist supporters and sympathisers, requiring a large garrison.

Malta was another problem; the British Army and RAF believed the island could not be held in the event of war with Italy. However the Royal Navy urged that everything possible should be done to retain the island, arguing that the fleet might be unable to fulfil its objective of severing Italian sea communications with North Africa and the position in the eastern Mediterranean could be endangered.[2] This attitude reflected that of Horatio Nelson, who on arriving in Grand Harbour in June 1803, wrote to the Admiralty: 'I now declare that I consider Malta as a most important outwork to India; and that it will give us great influence in the Levant, and indeed in all the southern ports of Italy. In this view, I hope we shall never give it up.'[3]

However, the Royal Navy was well aware in the event of war with Italy, Malta would no longer serve as a fleet base. If the fleet was deprived of the use of the island, it might be unable to control the passage through the central basin. The only port in the eastern Mediterranean that could accommodate a reasonably sized fleet was Alexandria, where many commercial facilities existed, and it would have to serve both as an operational and main base. It was far from ideal, being 800 miles from the Italian mainland and an almost equal distance to Malta, and the port itself was difficult to protect from the sea. There were questions too over oil fuel supply, ship repairs, docking facilities and general supplies. At Port Said there were the Shell Company's storage tanks, well situated, but at Alexandria the tanks were exposed and if bombed might result in the harbour waters being set on fire. It was therefore planned to keep 25,000 tons of fuel oil stored afloat in dispersed tankers, a wasteful use of these vital ships. They would replenish at Haifa where well situated storage tanks held 60,000 tons. Supply by an overland pipeline was thought to be far too vulnerable. Supply could also come via the Red Sea and Suez Canal, which might be targeted by the enemy but Cunningham was confident he could maintain this route.

The repair ship HMS *Resource* was berthed in Alexandria harbour, to conduct running repairs. Also destroyers and submarines had their own

repair and depot ships. However dockyard facilities were a pressing problem. There was only one graving dock (the classic form of drydock) in
the eastern Mediterranean capable of taking warships up to a 6-inch gun
cruiser of the *Arethusa* class. This was the Gabbari dock, owned by the
Egyptian Ports and Lights Administration, later taken over by the Admiralty
Dockyards. Docking was of vital importance, not only for repairs, but also
for cleaning the bottoms of ships. The weed growth that accumulated in
Alexandria harbour would soon reduce the speed of ships and would give
the Italians an advantage. Even by March 1939 the docking of capital ships
had still not been solved. It was suggested the Malta floating dock, capable
of docking the most modern battleships, should be moved to Alexandria.

The commander-in-chief objected, arguing the disadvantage of
losing Malta docking facilities altogether. Instead the Admiralty moved
the Portsmouth floating dock (A.F.D.5) to Alexandria where it arrived,
after an anxious voyage, only three weeks before the outbreak of war
with Germany. It had been built in 1912 and during the First World
War had served the Grand Fleet in Scottish waters. On arrival in
Alexandria the boilers had to be steamed and the machinery run continually throughout the whole period of the war, and at no point did
it break down. However it could only take vessels up to 31,500 tons,
which included *Queen Elizabeth* and *Royal Sovereign* class battleships in
a specially lightened condition but not more modern battleships. This
imposed limitations on the makeup of the Eastern Mediterranean Fleet.
The Malta floating dock was damaged in some of the first air raids of the
war, finally being put out of action and sunk in June 1940.[4]

Stores and victual supplies for the fleet had to be moved from Malta.
In January 1939 depots were set up in Alexandria and Port Said. With
the coming of war the main depot buildings covered three acres, which
rapidly grew to 30. The good dockside sheds were soon needed as transit
stores by all three services. The Royal Navy had to requisition other
buildings such as cotton warehouses, even an old church and racehorse
stables, which caused delays and security risks with stores scattered over
a wide area. It also led to a need for more transport, which the British
Army helped provide. Like fuel oil, reserve ammunition for the fleet was
stored afloat in merchant ships, while an underground magazine was
under construction in caves near Dekheila.

At the outbreak of war with Germany the Mediterranean Fleet was
drastically reduced, even though base facilities at Alexandria were well

in hand. Also before Italy entered the war Admiral Cunningham had transferred his flag ashore to Malta in November 1939. The battleships *Barham* and *Warspite* returned to UK waters, followed later by destroyers, depot and repair ships and MTBs. The battleship *Malaya* and aircraft carrier *Glorious* were sent to Aden to operate against raiders in the Indian Ocean. The heavy cruisers *Devonshire*, *Suffolk* and *Norfolk* joined the Home Fleet. By December the Mediterranean Fleet consisted of four light cruisers, an Australian destroyer flotilla and two submarines.

After Winston Churchill became Prime Minister the policy of withdrawal from the Mediterranean was reversed. Between April and June 1940 General Wavell received reinforcements from Australia and New Zealand and later South Africa. The Desert Army was reinforced with cruiser tanks and the RAF with Hurricane fighters and Wellington twin-engined bombers.

By May the British Mediterranean Fleet was back to near its pre-war strength of four battleships, eight 6-inch gun cruisers, 20 fleet destroyers and the old aircraft carrier *Eagle*. Also at Alexandria was a French squadron of one battleship, four cruisers and three destroyers.

Many of the battleships of all three nations in the Mediterranean were of First World War vintage. Only the four Italian ships and HMS *Warspite* had been modernised in the 1930s. For *Warspite* this involved new, lighter machinery and boilers, saving weight for additional armour protection and defensive weapons, and her main armament was updated. Reconstruction took three years involving completely gutting parts of the ship. She emerged from Portsmouth Dockyard in March 1937 virtually a new vessel, her major overhaul costing £2.3 million.[5]

In the western Mediterranean the French Fleet operating from bases at Toulon, Bizerta, Algiers and Oran was powerful, including two modern battlecruisers *Dunkerque* and *Strasbourg*, as well as two older battleships. At Gibraltar, under the Flag Officer, North Atlantic, which would later become Force H, was one British battleship, one light cruiser and nine destroyers.

The Italian fleet with their central position could concentrate superior force in the area of their choice, while being prepared for attacks from both directions. They had the advantage of speed over the British and more submarines than the Allies. However, a coordinated attack by the Allies would give them superior force, and the British had an aircraft carrier, though at that time her value was still unknown.

Admiral Cunningham was short of destroyers, a disadvantage he was to suffer through much of the early war in the Mediterranean. If he took his whole battle fleet to sea it severely restricted other activities. However he was still able to dominate the eastern basin, as long as there was a French fleet in the western basin.[6]

The morale of the Mediterranean Fleet was second to none and they were not disturbed by the coming of war. Indeed like the rest of the fleet, *Warspite* went to war while lying at anchor in Alexandria harbour, her crew enjoying rest and recreation.

> Lying in harbour was pretty boring for all the younger ratings, nothing to do ... Entertainment on board, except for the occasional film, consisted of the tannoy system. The favourite was, guess who, Vera Lynn. I will never forget Chamberlain's announcement of being at war with Germany. A lot of us congregated in the recreation space, some played games. Others got their heads down. When somebody switched on the tannoy speaker, a momentous time in history was nigh. But Jack was not impressed. By general consent the cry went up 'Shut that bloody thing off'.[7]

Admiral Cunningham received the news of the outbreak of war while watching the squadron regattas in Alexandria harbour from a 15-inch gun turret on *Malaya*. He was not surprised.

> There was little to be done. So far as possible all our preparations had been made. As I wrote to my aunt, I never expected when war was declared to have nothing to do but go ashore and have tea with my wife.
>
> We received the signal 'Winston is back', i.e. at the Admiralty, on the evening of September 3rd with considerable satisfaction.[8]

Notes
1 Cunningham, A.B. *A Sailor's Odyssey* p.241
2 Playfair, Major-General I.S.O. *The Mediterranean and Middle East Volume 1* p.30
3 Elliott, Peter, *The Cross and the Ensign. A naval history of Malta* p.69–70
4 Playfair, p.75–77
5 Plevy, Harry, *Battleship Sailors* p.100
6 Playfair, p.91–92
7 Stoker F.W. Earridge account, Imperial War Museum
8 Cunningham, p.217

4

Ultra Secret

Winston Churchill took office at the head of a coalition government on 10 May 1940, the day that the Phoney War ended and Germany began her western offensive Operation *Yellow*. He promised nothing but 'blood, toil, tears, and sweat.' His analysis was correct as Britain was brought to the brink of military disaster. Yet in one direction he was to have a significant advantage over the discredited Neville Chamberlain with the revival of fortunes in British intelligence. For, as fate would have it, the most valuable intelligence source in British history began to come online less than a fortnight after he became Prime Minister.

On 22 May the code breakers, recently relocated to Bletchley Park, broke the Luftwaffe version of the Enigma machine cipher, the Enigma being an electro-mechanical rotary machine that generated codes to encrypt messages. From that date onwards they were able to read German traffic almost without a break for the remainder of the war. 'Ultra' was the name used by the British for intelligence resulting from this decryption. Churchill called his Cryptanalysts 'the geese who laid the golden eggs and never cackled.'[1]

Ultra de-codes was an Allied rather than a purely British triumph, the culmination of years of intelligence work involving the Poles and the French as well as the British. The first breakthrough was made by Martin Rejewski, a brilliant mathematician from Posnan University who joined the cryptographic service of the Polish General Staff in 1932. By studying a commercial version of the Enigma machine and thousands of unsolved German intercepts, Rejewski succeeded in laying the theoretical foundations for the solution of Enigma.

All the Polish information and reconstructions of the Enigma machine and methods of decrypting ciphers were given by Polish Military Intelligence to the British and French on 26 July 1939, weeks before the German invasion of Poland. Bletchley Park cryptologist Gordon Welchman wrote 'Ultra would never have gotten off the ground if we had not learned from the Poles, in the nick of time, the details both of the German Military Enigma machine, and of the operating procedures that were in use.'[2] A year later in the early months of 1941 Bletchley Park had mastered the Naval Enigma.

Initially Army and RAF related material was compiled at Bletchley Park. The summaries were then distributed under the codeword 'Boniface'. The Admiralty produced its own intelligence summaries at the RN Operational Centre which were distributed under the codeword 'Hydro'.

From June 1941 the term 'Ultra Secret' was used; the codename 'Ultra' is said to have been the idea of Commander Geoffrey Colpays.[3] It was taken from the fact that the code-breaking success was considered more important than the highest security classification at the time (Most Secret) and so was regarded as being Ultra Secret.

It was under the irascible Admiral John Godfrey at Naval Intelligence in the legendary Room 39, that Ultra intercepts were interrupted. It was already a relic of an older statelier Admiralty. A large uncomfortable nineteenth-century office with high elaborate ceilings, iron radiators, cream coloured walls and a heavy black marble fireplace. The First Sea Lord had his office directly overhead; the private entrance to No 10 Downing Street was just visible on the opposite side of the square, and beyond that stretched the Foreign Office, the Treasury and the rest of Whitehall. Ian Fleming, celebrated author and creator of James Bond, was Godfrey's personal assistant. Throughout the war Room 39 was the nerve centre of the Naval Intelligence Division, originating, sifting and co-ordinating the day-to-day work.[4]

It was Godfrey, known as 'Uncle John' who saw Ewen Montague as having a natural ability for the work involving Ultra. He was soon running his own subsection along the corridor from Room 39, the top secret Section 17M, (M for Montague). This was in Room 13 where his small staff dealt with the Ultra intercepts. In the early years they came as a trickle, albeit a steady trickle, but grew to some 200 messages a day later in the war.

From Room 13 and Montague's team, information would find its way via the RN Operational Intelligence Centre – Section 8 as it was known – to ships at sea transmitted over normal naval radio circuits and protected by one time pad encryption.[5] Montague would later become famous for his part in Operation *Mincemeat* retold in his 1953 book *The Man who Never Was*.

The Allies became highly protective of the fact they had broken into the Enigma traffic.

> We got a huge series of messages with convoys carrying urgently needed petrol, ammunition, etc, across the Mediterranean to Rommel. These were included in the Orange Summaries because of their background value on whether Rommel could or could not carry out his plans, but they were dealt with operationally simultaneously by the O.I.C. These enabled us to sink a large proportion of these supplies than we could otherwise have done, and thus cripple Rommel's Army.
>
> Incidentally much praise is due to those who so managed our operations that they drained Rommel of supplies without compromising our sources of information; no naval sweep, no submarine patrol and no bombing flight was ordered to be at the right spot at the right time to intercept. Either one or several air reconnaissances sent to different areas – including, of course, the right one – sighted the German-Italian convoy first or seaborne sweeps were ordered which would 'just happen' to reach the right spot at the right time, on a neat piece of navigational planning.[6]

Orange Summaries were the summary of non-operational deciphered signals with comments provided to the First Sea Lord and the heads of naval operational staff twice a day by Section 17M. None of the operational ships, submarines or aircraft on reconnaissance knew they were working with the benefit on Ultra intercepts.[7]

On one occasion a convoy of five Italian ships sailed from Naples with vital supplies for the Afrika Korps. In this case there was no time for reconnaissance. The decision to attack solely on Ultra went directly to Churchill. The ships were all sunk by a precise attack arousing Axis suspicions. To cover this, a radio message was sent to a fictitious spy in Naples, congratulating him for his success, which it was known the Germans would be able to decode.

Ultra was to have a direct effect on the Battle of Matapan and several operations by the Royal Navy in the Mediterranean. During 1942, through Ultra intercepts, the British were able to foil German plans to sink British ships at Gibraltar using divers and limpet mines. Montague observed; 'The Italians on the other hand, had four successes in Gibraltar. But then we were not reading their messages!'[8] (Here Montague refers to radio traffic, not Enigma which was generally used by shore based command establishments.)

Notes

1   Andrew, Christopher, *Secret Service* p.449
2   Wetchman.G. p.289
3   West, Nigel, *GCHQ. The Secret Wireless War 1900–1986*
4   Pearson, John, *The Life of Ian Fleming* p.98–99
5   Beesly, Patrick, *Very Special Intelligence* p.142
6   Montague, Ewen, *Beyond Top Secret Ultra* p.100
7   Ibid p.181
8   Ibid p90

5

Early Clashes

The entry of Italy into the war and the collapse of France came roughly at the same time, presenting the British with several problems. The most pressing was to deal with the French Fleet while it was still crucial to retain Cunningham's fleet in the Eastern Mediterranean, which had the aim to seek out and destroy Italian naval forces. Cunningham found the news disturbing;

> Graver and graver became the news from France until, on June 24th, we heard she had capitulated to Germany and Italy. The next morning, when we were feeling rather depressed I was walking up and down the quarter-deck of the *Warspite*. I saw an Admiral's barge approaching, and went to the gangway to receive the Vice Admiral (D), John Tovey. A smiling figure ran up the gangway and greeted me with. 'Now I know we shall win the war, sir. We have no more allies!' Such depression as I had, vanished. It was impossible to feel downcast in the face of such optimism.[1]

Dealing with the fate of the French Fleet, their recent allies, was for the men involved a sad duty. Attempts to persuade the French to disperse their fleet to British, French overseas or American neutral ports met with limited success. Two old battleships, four destroyers, seven submarines and some smaller vessels reached British ports. Cunningham and his staff persuaded Rear-Admiral Godfrey at Alexandria, after much diplomacy, some arm twisting and veiled threats, to decommission his ships.

However the core of the French Fleet were dispersed by Admiral Jean Darlan, the French naval C-in-C; all he would say to his old allies were that the Germans and the Italians 'would not be allowed' to have the fleet.[2] However Churchill and the war cabinet felt unable to accept the risk of these ships falling into enemy hands. There was a large force in the Algerian Ports of Mers-el-Kebir and Oran. Force H at Gibraltar, under Vice Admiral Somerville was given the task of dealing with these vessels.

Force H had been formed partly to compensate for the loss of the French Mediterranean Fleet. It was able to lend support to the Atlantic or the western Mediterranean as required. At this point Somerville had the battlecruiser *Hood* and the battleships *Resolution* and *Valiant*, the carrier *Ark Royal*, two cruisers and eleven destroyers.

On the morning of 3 July Somerville's fleet arrived off the Algerian coast ready to put into action Operation *Catapult*. The former naval attaché at Paris, Captain C.S. Holland RN was sent ashore to see Admiral Gensoul, the French commander, with a six-hour ultimatum: to join the British, go into internment, sail to the French West Indies and disarm, scuttle their ships or be destroyed. Gensoul thought the British were bluffing and played for time so that his ships could raise steam.

Force H opened fire at 17:30. The battlecruiser *Strasbourg*, although sustaining some damage, and five destroyers, broke out and managed to reach Toulon. All other ships in the two ports were sunk or crippled within minutes. Stoker Vernon Coles, on board the destroyer HMS *Faulknor* witnessed the action.

> What a bombardment I had never seen anything like it. One of our destroyers out on the starboard wing had got too close inshore that she was coming under the range of their 9-inch gun.
>
> So the *Hood* just trained her guns to fire on the hill, just below a big fort which was where the firing was coming from. The fort came tumbling down because the blast had undermined its foundations. The French battleship *Dunkerque* was right under a dockyard crane and the *Hood* had to destroy it before she could get at *Dunkerque*. Her first broadside hit the crane; it was just like a matelot dropping. The second salvo hit the *Dunkerque*. We were firing from a distance of seven or eight miles, which for a 15-inch gun is point-blank range.[3]

The battleship *Bretagne* exploded and sank; 37 officers and 940 ratings were killed. Total casualties were 1,297 men killed.[4]

The next day at dawn, torpedo-carrying *Swordfish* aircraft from *Ark Royal* attacked the *Dunkerque* when doubts were raised over the extent of her damage. A torpedo hit on a tug alongside caused considerable hull damage to the battleship which put her out of action for a year.

In July, two convoys were waiting at Malta carrying men and stores required at Alexandria. The Italians were expected to try to intercept these ships, so the convoys would sail under the cover of a fleet operation. As a diversion Force H would cruise into the western Mediterranean and launch an air attack on Cagliari.

The fleet sailed from Alexandria on the evening of 7 July in three sections. Vice-Admiral Tovey led with the 7th Cruiser Squadron his flag-ship *Orion*, with *Neptune*, *Sydney*, *Gloucester* and *Liverpool*. Next came the fleet flagship *Warspite* with five destroyers. Behind that some miles astern were the slower battleships *Malaya* and *Royal Sovereign*, and the carrier *Eagle* (19 aircraft embarked) escorted by ten destroyers.

Several submarines were also patrolling the central basin. Early the next day the submarine *Phoenix* reported two Italian battleships and four destroyers in position between Benghazi and the toe of Italy cruising south. *Phoenix* never returned from this patrol. *Eagle's* air patrols sighted enemy submarines and bombed them.

The British fleet was soon subjected to several high-level air attacks over the next five days. During the course of one forenoon, observers on *Warspite* counted no fewer than 300 bombs dropped round her in 22 attacks, the closest when 24 bombs fell close along the port side while at the same time twelve close across the starboard bow, and all within 200 yards of the ship.[5] Admiral Cunningham was complimentary of the Regia Aeronautica:

> To us at the time it appeared that they had some squadrons specially trained for anti-ship work. Their reconnaissance was highly efficient, and seldom failed to find and report our ships at sea. The bombers invariably arrived within an hour or two. They carried out high-level attacks from about 12,000 feet, pressed home in formation in the face of the heavy anti-aircraft fire of the fleet, and for this type of attack their accuracy was very good. We were fortunate to escape being hit.[6]

On the evening of the 8th one of Tovey's ships, the *Gloucester*, was hit, the bomb falling on the bridge, killing the captain and seventeen other men.

Reports from a flying boat late in the afternoon indicated to Cunningham that the Italian force now consisted of 2 battleships, 6 cruisers and 7 destroyers, and was about 60 miles north of Benghazi steering northwest.

Commander Bragadin reveals that the Italian fleet was constantly shadowed by British reconnaissance aircraft. Yet, 'Italian reconnaissance did not succeed even in locating the enemy formation. This failure left both Supermarina and Admiral Campioni with many grave doubts, extending even to the point of wondering whether the British ships might have withdrawn toward Alexandria.'[7]

This is an odd statement since the British fleet had been under heavy air attack from aircraft all day. It points to a severe lack of communication between the Regia Marina and Regia Aeronautica, if one had no idea of the location of the enemy the other was attacking.

However in contrast Cunningham's reconnaissance was working well; another report indicated the Italian fleet hand changed course to the east. This convinced him the enemy were covering convoys to Libya; this, combined with the heavy air attacks on the fleet, caused him to postpone the sailing of the eastbound Malta convoys. His fleet worked up to their best speed to get between the enemy and his base at Taranto and bring them to battle.

At 06:00 on 9 July *Warspite* was some 60 miles west of Navarino. Leading were Tovey's cruisers, eight miles astern *Warspite*, and a similar distance further back the slower battleships and the carrier *Eagle*.

Two hours later the enemy fleet was reported about 145 miles ahead by flying boats from No 228 Squadron RAF, consisting of two battleships, 16–18 cruisers, and 25–30 destroyers, an accurate report as it turned out. At 13:30 nine *Swordfish* torpedo bombers of No 824 Squadron from *Eagle* made their first strike but were unable to find the battleships and attacked a cruiser instead with no success.[8] Campioni quickly grasped the fact the aircraft must have come from a carrier. Reconnaissance aircraft were launched from his fleet which soon found the British 80 miles away. The Italian fleet set course toward them.

At about 14:15 Cunningham's fleet had reached a favourable position between the enemy and the Italian base of Taranto, so he altered course due west. Contact was imminent; it would be the first clash between the British and Italian fleets.

It was not quite the moment I would have chosen to give battle. They had a large number of cruisers, and we, because of the damaged *Gloucester* which was not fit to fight in serious fighting, had no more than four, which had little more than 50% of their ammunition remaining. Moreover, the speed of approach was limited by the maximum speed of the *Royal Sovereign*.[9]

Cunningham ordered *Gloucester* back to support *Eagle*, while *Warspite* strained to catch up with the cruisers.

At 14:47 the enemy was sighted by *Orion*. The Italians opened fire about 30 minutes later. Admiral Tovey's four ships were heavily outnumbered, out-gunned and out-ranged. However *Warspite* came into action at 15:26, the enemy cruisers turning away under a smoke screen. A lull followed in the action.

At 15:50 *Warspite* sighted the two *Cavour* class battleships and both sides exchanged fire at 26,000 yards. Shooting was good, both sides obtaining straddles. A few minutes later a hit was observed at the base of the leading Italian battleship's foremost funnel. This resulted in a fire below decks which extinguished some boilers. The vessel in question, *Cesare* the flagship, lost speed and dropped to 19 knots. The heavy cruiser *Bolzano* was also hit by three 6-inch shells with no effect to her speed or fighting efficiency.

On the British side only the cruiser *Neptune* received some light damage from a near miss. The Italians thought they had hit *Warspite*; from the *Cesare* they could see flames around the rear turrets. However it was only one of her catapult aircraft that had caught fire from the flash of the ship's own guns and her crew dumped the aircraft over the side.

Under smokescreens Campioni withdrew his battleships, aware he faced three enemy battleships. Destroyers covered the withdrawal, the battleships moving southwest while the destroyers conducted an ineffective torpedo attack.

Eagle also launched another air strike which was unsuccessful. British destroyers counterattacked with cruiser support but came under heavy fire from enemy ships covering the retiring battleships.

At about 16:40 Cunningham broke off the action, concerned about submarine and or destroyer ambushes.

I had no intention of plunging straight into the enemy smoke-screen. We decided to work around to the windward and to the northward of it. Some of our destroyers were clear of it by 5 o'clock, but the enemy were out of sight.[10]

Indeed Campioni's plan had been to try and lure the British across a line of submarines using his superior speed. However the submarines were too far south.

By this time the British fleet was only 25 miles from the coast of Calabria. More high-level bombing attacks developed over the next four hours, during which the Regia Aeronautica even managed to bomb their own fleet – much to the fury of Campioni – although failing to hit any ships.

Admiral Cunningham was not altogether happy with the outcome:

> The action was most unsatisfactory to us. I suppose it was too much to expect the Italians to stake everything on a stand-up fight. Yet if they had timed their attacks better with all types of arms they employed they might have given us much trouble. The one 15-inch hit they sustained from the *Warspite* had a morale effect quite out of proportion to the damage.[11]

The Italians commander as you might expect, saw it rather differently:

> An objective analysis of the engagement must reach the conclusion that the results were about equal. No ship was sunk; the four hits suffered by the Italian ships had no serious consequences and the same was true of the damage suffered by the *Neptune* and *Warspite*. Both sides succeeded in the primary purpose for which they had taken to sea; that is, to get their respective through convoys to their destinations. Each failed to prevent the operations of the other because neither understood the other's purposes soon enough.[12]

It should be pointed out the Regia Marina at that time only had two operational battleships available. It would be another month before the new battleships *Littorio* and *Vittorio Veneto* entered service. Therefore their cautious approach in this action is perhaps understandable.

So ended the action off Calabria; the Italians called it Punto Stilo. Undoubtedly Cunningham did establish a 'moral ascendancy' over the Italian fleet, and had proved his fleet could operate in the central basin

Aegean
Sea

GREECE

Athens
Piraeus

Peloponnese

C. Matapan

Crete

EAGLE
1st air strike, 11:45

1st strike, 14:00

Brief action between
surface forces, 16:00–16:45.
Both sides withdraw

ITALY

Calabria

Messina

Syracuse

Sicily

Malta

MEDITERRANEAN SEA

100 sea miles

0

Action of Calabria, 9 July 1940

– – – Italian fleet returning to Taranto after escorting convoy

——— British fleet on route to Malta

even against the combined surface ships, air power and submarines of the enemy.

As the Italian fleet moved toward the straits of Messina, Cunningham's fleet turned toward Malta. That night an air strike launched from *Eagle* attacked shipping in Augusta harbour on Sicily where they hoped to find heavy units of the Regia Marina. However the harbour was largely empty but for a tanker and the destroyer *Pancaldo*, which were both sunk.

For the next 24 hours Cunningham's fleet cruised to the south and east of Malta, while the *Royal Sovereign* and destroyers entered harbour to fuel. The Vice-Admiral Malta, learning the fleets were engaged, had used the window of opportunity to sail the convoys to Alexandria. While they were attacked by Italian aircraft, no ships were hit. By 12 July they were under the air umbrella of the Desert Air Force, and Blenheim fighters of No 252 Squadron chased off the enemy bombers. The next morning the fast convoy arrived, followed two days later by the slow convoy.

At first Mussolini was delighted with the results of the clash at Punto Stilo, no doubt influenced by the exaggerated claims of the Regia Aeronautica, which stated on Rome Radio that they had 'annihilated 50 per cent of the British naval power in the Mediterranean.' Ciano thought differently and wrote in his diary on 13 July that 'The real controversy in the naval conflicts is not between us and the British, but between our air force and our navy.' The claimed numbers of British losses he judged to be 'somewhat exaggerated'.[13]

Cunningham was delighted that his wife and two nieces had got out of Malta on the fast convoy. On the island they had been

> Bombed practically every night and often by day, they had not enjoyed it. My wife had chalked up seventy-two raids from the day Italy entered the war until the time she left, a period of twenty-nine days ... [I found them] a flat about six miles out from Alexandria where they could hear and see the bombs and gunfire when the raids took place.[14]

Alexandria (Aleck), air raids and all, became the home port of thousands of matelots over the war years. Charles Causley, poet and writer, a PO coder at the time wrote:

Aleck. Ah, I can remember thinking; here it is at last, the real thing; Anthony and Cleopatra, guidebook by E.M. Forster, brilliant blue sea. Pharaohs, Alexander the Great, Stewart Grainger!

Of course, the locals soon put a stop to all that: but I still think it was an exciting prospect. And, meanwhile, Tug and I prepared for our run ashore, changing English money into ackers and putting on our number sixes – those flashing white sailor-suits that made us look as if we only needed a balloon or a toy windmill in hand to complete the picture.

The run ashore did not live up to expectations.

We did the usual round; tombola at the Fleet Club, the pictures sending home boxes of horrible-looking marshmallows, buying cameras that wouldn't photograph, pens that wouldn't write and watches that fell to pieces as soon as you wound them up. I liked the rows of clean white books in the French bookshops, the elegant faces of the Greek women, and the iced coffee we got at the Rio bar. And, like all mate-lots, we ended up in the bar of the Blue Anchor Club, where we'd booked beds for the night, drinking John Collinses, eating peanuts and listening to an Egyptian band tearing the life out of a selection from *Follow the Fleet*.[15]

Cunningham rightly could claim victory in the action off Calabria but it had revealed limitations in his fleet:

Several serious implications had arisen, and perhaps the most important was that the 25-year old *Warspite*, which had been reconstructed and modernised, was the only ship in the fleet which could shoot at the ranges at which Italian battleships and 8-inch gun cruisers were straddling us comfortably. In writing privately to the First Sea Lord on the day of our arrival I pointed out this fact, and that during the first clash with the Italians neither the *Malaya* nor *Royal Sovereign* crossed the target. I must have at least one more ship that can shoot at a good range.[16]

Admiral Pound was quick to respond to the problem. The Mediterranean Fleet was sent the 8-inch gun cruiser *Kent*, but lost the

Royal Sovereign which went to Durban, South Africa for badly needed repairs. Other substantial reinforcements were on the way; *Warspite*'s sister ship the modernised *Valiant*, together with the new fleet aircraft carrier *Illustrious* and the anti-aircraft cruisers *Calcutta* and *Coventry* came from Britain. Assembling at Gibraltar they left there on 30 August in company with Force H consisting of the battlecruiser *Renown*, aircraft carrier *Ark Royal*, cruiser *Sheffield* and seven destroyers for the central Mediterranean.

The Eastern Fleet also left Alexandria on 30 August consisting of *Warspite*, *Malaya*, *Eagle*, two cruisers and nine destroyers to receive the additional ships. A convoy of an oil tanker and two merchant ships left Alexandria at the same time for Malta with an escort of four destroyers.

On 31 August air reconnaissance spotted vessels of the Regia Marina at sea, reporting 2 battleships, 7 cruisers and 8 destroyers steering south toward Cunningham's fleet 130 miles away. However the force was in fact more substantial than reported. The modernised *Duilio* had entered service and *Cesare*'s damage from Calabria had been repaired. Also at sea were *Cavour* and the new battleships *Littorio* and *Vittorio Veneto*; the latter ships had a similar profile to some heavy cruisers in the Italian fleet.

Cunningham's first priority was the convoy so he remained to the south. Late on 31 August the Italian fleet reversed its course, with orders to resume the southerly course in the morning. During the night a severe storm boiled up from the north preventing air reconnaissance in the morning.

On 2 September the reinforcements joined the Eastern Fleet. The adverse weather still prevented flying. When Supermarina in Rome learned of the presence of the additional ships in Alexandria harbour, they assumed they must have arrived via the Red Sea.[17]

Late in September 1940 Cunningham's reinforced fleet escorted some convoys and transported troops to Malta. Two thousand soldiers were embarked on the cruisers *Liverpool* and *Gloucester,* while *Warspite*, *Valiant*, and *Illustrious* supplied the heavy escort. They were heavily bombed but Fulmer fighters from *Illustrious* took a toll on the raiders. To the north the Italian fleet was spotted at sea with four battleships, but they did not try to interfere with the movement.

Early in October a convoy of supplies from Alexandria was run through to the beleaguered island. This time it was covered by the entire fleet, reaching Malta without incident; fortunately the weather was bad so they did not suffer the usual attentions of the Regia Aeronautica.

On the night of 11/12 October the fleet escorted a small convoy away from Malta. The cruiser *Ajax*, patrolling to the north, ran into an Italian destroyer flotilla. Supermarina was operating blind as usual, but after a report from a civilian aircraft en route to Libya that the British fleet was at sea, they sent out a night patrol of six destroyers and four motor torpedo boats to the northeast of Malta. Another patrol was sent out to the west of the island in case it was Force H.

On the eastern patrol at 01:35 the destroyer *Alciane* spotted an enemy cruiser which at first began to flash recognition signals, while the destroyer attacked with torpedoes. Cunningham described the action involving *Ajax*.

> After a most spirited action at ranges of 4,000 yards and less in the moonlight she sank two destroyers and damaged a third, setting her on fire. She then engaged two other ships, which disappeared behind a smoke screen with some celerity when fire was opened. The *Ajax* did not come off unscathed. Hit seven times in all she sustained considerable damage to her bridge and radar equipment, largely caused by a fire in a storeroom. There was some difficulty in the *Ajax* because of the blinding effect of the flash of her own guns, whereas the enemy was using flashless ammunition with good tracers.[18]

The destroyer *Artigliere* was sunk later that day by the cruiser *York*, after she was found dead in the water. Floats were dropped in the water for her crew before she was finished off with torpedoes.

Radar came as a surprise to Commander Bragadin:

> it had to be admitted that the Italians were technically inferior to the British, at least as far as carrying out night encounters at sea was concerned. In reality this inferiority was probably to be explained solely by the fact that the *Ajax* was equipped with radar, while the Italians did not yet know the British had succeeded in perfecting that device to the point where it could be used in operations. This existence of combat worthy enemy radar was not known to the Italians until after the battle of Cape Matapan in March 1941.[19]

Notes

1 Cunningham, A.B. *A Sailor's Odyssey* p.238
2 Van Der Vat, Dan, *Standard of Power. The Royal Navy in the Twentieth Century* p.199
3 Arthur, Max, *Lost Voices of the Royal Navy* p.256
4 Playfair, Major-General I.S.O. *The Mediterranean and Middle East Volume 1* p.136
5 Ibid p.151
6 Cunningham, p.258
7 Bragadin, M.A. *The Italian Navy in World War II* p.28
8 Playfair, p.153
9 Cunningham, p.259
10 Ibid p.262
11 Ibid p.263
12 Bragadin, p.29
13 Ciano, G. *Ciano's Diary 1937–1943* p.370
14 Cunningham, p.264–265
15 Causley, Charles, *Hands to Dance and Skylark* p.29–30
16 Cunningham, p.26
17 Bragadin, p.33
18 Cunningham, p.278
19 Bragadin, p.39–40

6

Operation Judgement

HMS *Illustrious* was laid down in April 1937, launched in April 1939 and completed fitting out a year later. After trials at Bermuda and a minor refit where some problems were ironed out, she sailed for the Mediterranean and joined Admiral Cunningham's fleet.

Illustrious was the class leader of six aircraft carriers and was markedly different to the carriers that had gone before. She was heavily armoured on her flight deck and on the hanger deck, displacing 23,000 tons, 28,000 tons under full load, with a speed of 30 knots. Later ships in the class would be even larger. However she carried fewer aircraft than *Ark Royal* which had double hangers; this was mainly due to the armour and a shorter flight deck. Anti-aircraft defence was much improved having sixteen 4.5inch anti-aircraft guns in eight turrets. She could accommodate 36 aircraft.

Charles Lamb joined the new *Illustrious* with the rest of 815 Squadron as a Swordfish pilot.

I had never been on board a purpose built aircraft carrier before and was most impressed I could only make comparisons with the old *Courageous,* but everything in *Illustrious* was so much bigger and better that the comparison was absurd.

Courageous had been converted into a carrier from the hull of an old cruiser but this ship had sprung into life from the combined skills of many marine architects. The result was not just a masterpiece of planning and design, but a mighty ship of great beauty. Comparing her with *Courageous* was tantamount to comparing her with Noah's Ark.[1]

The Royal Navy at that time had the best design of aircraft carriers available. With their armoured flight decks they were able to withstand far more punishment than vessels in service with the US Navy or the Imperial Japanese Navy, although they carried fewer aircraft and those aircraft were outdated.

The mainstay of the Fleet Air Arm was the Swordfish aircraft, first flown in 1934 and entering service in 1936, it was a jack of all trades with six roles: reconnaissance, spotting for the guns of the fleet, convoy escort-anti submarine, torpedo strike aircraft, dive bombing and mine laying. A Swordfish was powered by a single Bristol Pegasus engine providing 690hp. It carried a crew of three men, each in his own open cockpit, a pilot, observer and telegraphist air gunner in the rear. Range was 450nm but this could be increased with additional fuel tanks to about 900nm at the cost of one crew member. Armament consisted of two Vickers machine guns, one fired by the pilot through the propeller in First World War style, the other used by the rear gunner. A variety of ordnance could be carried, something for every occasion, a single 18inch MK XIIB 1,620lb torpedo, four 250lb depth charges, 500lb or 250lb bombs up to 1,500lbs, or six rockets. The maximum speed was 125 knots although few pilots managed this; in normal level flight around 90 was normal.

It was from the variety of ordnance the Swordfish could carry that it got its affectionate nickname, when some test pilot observed: 'No housewife on a shopping spree could cram a wider variety of articles into her string bag.' However the String Bag was sturdy and robust and able to fly with a high degree of damage.

> Nevertheless there was never any doubt that the String Bag was a very slow machine, and a vulnerable target for all, especially in daylight … the lumbering old ladies were an easy prey for a capable fighter pilot, providing he appreciated the remarkable manoeuvrability of the old biplane he was attacking.[2]

The Fairy Fulmar carried by *Illustrious* was a big advance on earlier Fleet Air Arm fighter aircraft, even monoplanes like the Blackburn Skua. However it was far from ideal, its two-man crew affected performance even though it used the same engine as the Spitfire and Hurricane, the Rolls-Royce Merlin. It first flew in January 1937, entering service in

1940. It had a speed of 230 knots, about 100 knots less than a Spitfire. It carried eight 0.303 Browning machine guns, and in a fighter bomber role could carry two 250lb bombs. Its rate of climb was slow because it was heavy but it was the best fighter the Royal Navy had, and against Italian aircraft it was to prove adequate.

Illustrious brought another advantage to Cunningham's force: she had the best radar of any ship in that fleet. Fighters could be directed onto enemy aircraft; thus 806 Squadron – even though they only had Fulmars – would make a significant difference.

Captain Denis Boyd, commanding officer of *Illustrious*, told his men:

> Mussolini has become boastful; he has got into the habit of referring to the Mediterranean as 'Mare Nostrum' which means 'our sea'. We are going to change it to 'Cunningham's Pond'.[3]

On 28 October 1940 Italy invaded Greece unprovoked. The next day Ciano wrote in his diary 'Diplomatic reactions in the Balkans are quite limited for the time being. No one makes a move to defend the Greeks.'[4]

On 5 November Winston Churchill told the House of Commons: 'We have most carefully abstained from any action likely to draw upon the Greeks the enmity of the criminal dictators. For their part the Greeks have maintained so strict a neutrality that we were unacquainted with their dispositions or their intentions.' Britain deployed forces to Crete to establish naval fuelling facilities and a cruiser took a battalion of infantry there to help establish a forward base.

All units of the Eastern Mediterranean Fleet were recalled to fuel, while air reconnaissance over Greece and the Ionian Sea from Malta was intensified. On 29 October Cunningham's whole fleet put to sea; four battleships, two aircraft carriers, four cruisers and three destroyer flotillas swept into the Ionian Sea. They found no sign of the Italians. In fact the Italians had planned an operation for landings on Corfu, but this was cancelled and the forces involved switched to landing at Valona in Albania.

Air reconnaissance reported the Italian fleet to be at Taranto and Brindisi. *Warspite* and *Illustrious* returned to Alexandria on 2 November. The rest of the fleet returned the next day.

The Regia Marina, although not entirely in the dark, was not told officially of the decision to invade Greece until 16 October. According to Commander Bragadin:

The Navy's view was that the proposed move would worsen, among other things, the strategic situation in the east-central Mediterranean and in the Ionian Sea.

Further this undertaking would put the Italian garrison in the Dodecanese Islands in serious difficulties and would split the navy's forces even more.

The Italians' Greek campaign soon degenerated into a shambles, much of it due to poor planning. The Albanian ports did not have the capacity to supply the armies, as they were only able to handle 3,500 tons of supplies a day; the Italian Army needed 10,000 tons. Soon the port of Durazzo was congested with 70 ships waiting to unload while 30,000 tons of supplies were piled on the docks.[5]

General Wavell, after a meeting of the Defence Committee, was authorised to send a further infantry brigade to defend the Greek Islands and Suda Bay on Crete in particular. An infantry battalion would be sent out via Gibraltar to Wavell, along with reinforcements for Malta and the Eastern Fleet; this was while Operation *Sea Lion* still remained a possibility at home.

During October and the early days of November there was a great deal of traffic through the waters of the Mediterranean, as men and materiel were ferried from Italy to Albania. British convoys moved from their main bases to outposts around Greece in the Aegean Sea. Most Italian moves were beyond the striking distance of British forces; however the Royal Navy and its convoys were subjected to continuous raids by the Regia Aeronautica. And all the time Admiral Campioni was waiting at Taranto to pounce on any weak detachment if it strayed within his range.

Admiral Cunningham had for some time considered attacking the Italian battle fleet in their harbour at Taranto. By October 1940 there were six battleships there with numerous cruisers and destroyers, safe from surface attack. The planned raid on Taranto had been about for several years. First hatched in 1935 when Italy invaded Abyssinia, the then C-in-C Mediterranean Fleet Admiral Sir William Wordsworth Fisher had planned to use aircraft from the carrier *Glorious* to attack the fleet at Taranto, but at the time Britain took no action.

Three years later in March 1938, tension was high again when Hitler annexed Austria. Admiral Sir Dudley Pound then commanded in the Mediterranean, while on board *Glorious* was Captain Lumley St George

Lyster who was to become one of the mainstays of the Fleet Air Arm. His squadrons had become highly proficient at night flying.

With the help of his Commander Flying, Guy Willougby and the senior observer Commander Lachlan Mackintosh, they revised the 1935 plan, while the three Swordfish squadrons conducted intensive training. The crisis passed and the plan was locked away in a safe aboard the *Glorious,* and may have gone to the bottom with her when she was sunk off Norway.

Lyster had arrived with *Illustrious* as Rear Admiral Carriers. Cunningham wrote of his first meeting with him.

> At our first interview he brought up the matter of an attack on the Italian fleet in Taranto harbour, and I gave him every encouragement to develop the idea. It had, of course, already been mentioned in my correspondence with Sir Dudley Pound, though to him the operation always appeared as the last dying kick of the Mediterranean carrier before being sent to the bottom. To Admiral Lyster and myself the project seemed to involve no unusual danger.[6]

So Operation *Judgement* was born. The RAF increased reconnaissance flights over Taranto providing photographs of the two harbours – the large outer harbour Mar Grande, and the smaller inner harbour Mar Piccolo – the defences and shore facilities. Both carriers were to be used in the operation. The date was set as 21 October, Trafalgar Day, although the fact it was a moonlit night was more pertinent.

It was almost as if once the date of the operation was set the fates turned against the Fleet Air Arm. The Swordfish aircraft had to be fitted with long range tanks to enable them to reach Taranto while keeping the carrier out of harm's way, which were fitted into the middle cockpit thus reducing the crew and moving the observer to the rear cockpit. While the modification work was being carried out on *Illustrious* a fire broke out; the sprinkler system on the hanger deck saved most of the aircraft, but two were burnt out, while five others were damaged by fire and the salt water from the sprinklers. All the aircraft had to be stripped down and rebuilt, after being cleaned with fresh water. Even though many members of the squadrons helped with the work, there was no alternative but to postpone the raid to 31 October which would make it more difficult as there would be limited moonlight.

It was only realised days before the raid was due that it would now depend much more on light from flares. They had to get it right; there would be no second chance. So it was postponed again to the next moonlit night, 11/12 November.

The carriers would leave Alexandria with the rest of the fleet to cover convoys to Greece, Crete and Malta. A good cover for the operation for secrecy was vital. Force H would come into the western basin attacking Cagliari with aircraft from *Ark Royal*. Convoy MW3 would sail from Alexandria to Malta and the empty ships ME3 from Malta to Alexandria. Also the battleship *Barham*, cruisers *Glasgow* and *Berwick* and six destroyers after dropping troops at Malta would move through to join the Mediterranean Fleet.

On 4 November the first of the convoys began. However, ill fate struck again. The carrier *Eagle* had suffered numerous near misses in Italian bombing raids but this strain led to a breakdown in the ship's aviation fuel system, and her ageing boilers were troublesome. Further delays were out of the question with winter weather approaching. Like many of the Royal Navy's ships, *Eagle* was old and due to operational demands long overdue a refit. Without *Eagle* it meant 24 aircraft would now be available instead of 30; this included six aircraft transferred from *Eagle* to *Illustrious*.

On 6 November *Illustrious* set sail from Alexandria accompanied by four battleships as well as cruisers and destroyers. Her Fulmars providing air cover for the fleet and convoys. Charles Lamb recalled the final briefing for the Swordfish crews on board *Illustrious*.

> In the wardroom a large scale map of Taranto and a magnificent collection of enlarged prints of the photographs I had brought out from Malta were pinned to cardboard backings and on display. It was possible to study every aspect of the harbour and its defences, and the balloons; and, of course all the ships in detail.

All the Italian capital ships and some of the heavy cruisers were protected by anti-torpedo nets, hung from booms, shielding the ships down to the keels. However the torpedoes carried by the Swordfish were fitted with Duplex Pistols, a magnetic device which would explode on contact or would be activated by the ship's magnetic field. The torpedoes to be used were set to pass under the hulls avoiding the nets.[7]

The use of torpedoes made the operation hazardous, as the aircraft would be forced to come in low. The dropping area was known to be restricted by balloons; for this reason no more than six torpedo-bombers were to be used at a time. The attack would be formed in two waves an hour apart. In each wave there would be two aircraft dropping flares to the east of the anchorage to light up the battleships. Also, more as a diversion, bombing attacks would be made on the inner harbour.

However bad luck had still not deserted the British forces. Swordfish aircraft maintained reconnaissance patrols, in particular on the lookout for enemy submarines as the fleet steamed west. On 10 November one of 819's Swordfish, an *Illustrious* aircraft, had its engine cut out 20 miles from the ship. The pilot tried to glide the aircraft back to the carrier but it was too far and the plane crashed in the sea. Both crewmen were picked up, returning to *Illustrious* in a cruiser's Walrus aircraft. One aircraft suffering engine failure was not that unusual, but the next morning another aircraft suffered the same fate. It was quickly found that one of the ship's aviation fuel tanks had been contaminated by seawater, probably due to the hanger fire and the use of the sprinkler system. All aircraft to be used on Operation *Judgement* had their fuel systems drained and refuelled.

By the late afternoon of 11 November the latest aerial photographs were flown to *Illustrious*; they showed five battleships in the outer harbour, and a flying boat had reported a sixth entering. They were about 200 miles from the target. Fulmers shot down two Italian spotter planes which might have raised the alarm but did not, as they were no doubt surprised by the fighters directed onto them by the radar on *Illustrious*.

Admiral Cunningham signalled *Illustrious* about 18:00, along with her cruisers and destroyers to proceed with 'orders for Operation *Judgement*. Good luck then to your lads in their enterprise. Their success may well have a most important bearing on the course of the war in the Mediterranean.'[8]

Two hours later *Illustrious* was 40 miles 270° from Kabbo Point, Cephalonia, and 170 miles from the target.

Shortly before 20:30 the first wave of Swordfish from 813, 815, and 824 Squadrons led by Lieutenant-Commander Kenneth Williamson started lumbering off the flight deck of *Illustrious* with their heavy loads, clawing at the air to gain height. Williamson led them up into cloud at 4,500 feet, turning toward the west and immediately lost contact with the others. At 7,500 feet he emerged into clear moonlight to find he

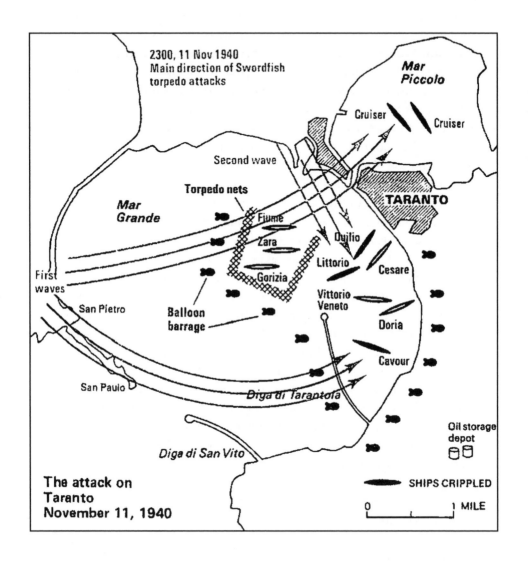

2300, 11 Nov 1940
Main direction of Swordfish
torpedo attacks

Mar Piccolo

Cruiser

Cruiser

Second wave

Torpedo nets

Mar Grande

Fiume

Zara

Oujlio

Gorizia

Littorio

TARANTO

Cesare

First waves

San Pietro

Balloon barrage

Vittorio Veneto

Doria

Cavour

San Paulo

Diga di Tarantola

Oil storage depot

Diga di San Vito

The attack on
Taranto
November 11, 1940

SHIPS CRIPPLED

0   1 MILE

had lost four aircraft, he was not overly concerned it was accepted they would make their own way to the target 90 minutes flying time away.

The second strike led by Lieutenant-Commander J.W. 'Ginger' Hale CO of 819 Squadron took off an hour later. His flight was reduced to eight aircraft, five armed with torpedoes, the others with bombs and flares.

Charles Lamb's aircraft L5B was a flare dropper; from 50 miles out they could see lights from the harbour. As they got closer the defences came to life.

> The sky over the harbour looked like it sometimes does over Mount Etna, in Sicily, when the great volcano erupts. The darkness was being torn apart by a firework display which spat flame into the night to a height of nearly 5,000 feet.[9]

Just before 23:00 the flare droppers and bombers of the first wave left formation for their tasks; all aircraft had rendezvoused at the target.

The moon was three-quarters full, and to the east flares were brightly illuminating the battleships ahead as the torpedo bombers peeled off to the westward for their final approach. The two sub-flights of three came in toward the anchorage across Cape Rondinella and San Pietro Island, dropping down to 30 feet skimming across the water. Anti-aircraft fire flashed toward them from shore batteries and the ships.

The first aircraft attacked the southernmost battleship, the *Cavour*, the torpedo struck home but the aircraft was badly damaged and crashed into the water near the floating dock.

A minute later *Littorio* was struck under the starboard bow by a torpedo from the second flight. Minutes later she was hit again on the port quarter. The other torpedoes from the first wave missed, exploded prematurely, or failed to go off. The flare dropping aircraft, having completed their primary task, switched to bombing the oil storage tanks, while other bombers swooped on the ships in the inner harbour, mostly cruisers and destroyers, where they were moored with sterns against the jetty.

The approach of the second wave was the same. The five torpedo-bombers came in and struck the *Duilio* on the starboard side and hit the *Littorio* again; a fourth hit on this ship failed to explode.

Lieutenant Michael Torrens-Spence, Swordfish torpedo-bomber pilot:

During the attack a hundred thousand rounds were fired at us but only one aircraft was shot down in each wave. I got hit underneath by one half-inch machine gun bullet. It was the pilot's job to aim the torpedo. Nobody was given a specific target. I dived down in between the moored ships aimed at the nearest big one, which turned out to be the *Littorio*, and released my torpedo. While you're low down over the water and surrounded by enemy ships the comfort is that they can't shoot at you without shooting each other. I then made for the entrance to the harbour at zero feet and thence back to *Illustrious*.[10]

The *Vittorio Veneto* and the heavy cruiser *Gorizia* were attacked but escaped unscathed. The Italians, as Lieutenant Torrens-Spence indicated, had a great dilemma firing at aircraft only 30 feet above the surface of the harbour, as it meant hitting their own ships and the town and harbour facilities of Taranto. Generally they lifted their angle of fire. Had they maintained fire at water level it is possible few aircraft would have reached their targets, instead of only two being shot down.

The first wave, less one aircraft, arrived back on board *Illustrious* four and a half hours after taking off. The one aircraft lost was that of their leader Williamson, who with his observer was taken prisoner. By 03:00 the second wave, also less one aircraft, was back on board. Swordfish E4H was lost, shot down attacking the cruiser *Gorizia*. Lieutenants A. Bayley and H.J. Slaughter were both killed when their aircraft blew up. Bayley's body was found after the war and buried at Taranto; it was later moved to the military cemetery at Bari, and there maintained by the Commonwealth War Graves Commission. Slaughter's body was never recovered.[11]

During the next day, 12 November, Italian aircraft tried to locate the British fleet, and in particular *Illustrious*. Some of these aircraft were shot down by Fulmars, and they failed to find any ships. It had been intended to repeat the attack the next night but weather conditions deteriorated. However that night ten RAF Wellington bombers from Malta attacked the inner harbour and set the Agip oil tanks on fire.[12]

Air reconnaissance photographs over Taranto showed the *Cavour* beached. The *Littorio* and *Duilio* were seriously damaged. It looked like two cruisers had been hit by bombs.

The first Supermarina had known of the raid was when they received frantic telephone calls from Taranto. Commander Bragadin was on duty in the operations room at Rome that night. 'Bulletin followed on bulletin. It seemed that a great naval battle had been lost, and no one yet knew if and when it would be possible to recover from the grave consequences of it.'

Salvage work was quickly underway at Taranto.

> The *Littorio* and *Duilio* were 'out of danger' within a few days and were sent to ship yards for repair. Moving the *Littorio* was a particularly delicate operation because divers discovered an unexploded torpedo in the mud under the keel.[13]

Littorio and *Duilio* were rapidly repaired and ready for sea by May 1941. The *Cavour* could not be refloated until July 1941, and then she was towed to Trieste for repair, but this had not been completed by the armistice in 1943.

The main objective of the British attack had been successfully achieved. Half the Italian battle fleet had been put out of action, albeit temporarily. *Illustrious* soon rejoined the fleet to be welcomed by a signal from the flagship. '*Illustrious* manoeuvre well executed.'[14]

Italian losses of the night of 11/12 November were not confined to Taranto. Admiral Pridham-Wippell had taken his cruisers and destroyers north, raiding the convoy route between Albania and Italy. A convoy of four merchantmen heading for Brindisi was sighted with two escorts; a short action followed in which all four ships were sunk.

The Taranto raid made a profound impression around the world; here was proof that a fleet was not safe in harbour. The effect on the balance of power in the Mediterranean was immediate, for all major Italian warships left Taranto for more secure ports on the west coast of Italy, thus reducing the threat to British convoy routes through the Mediterranean and to Greece.

Winston Churchill announced to the House of Commons that the Fleet Air Arm had 'annihilated the Italian fleet forever.' Something of an exaggeration but it was one of Britain's first victories and a welcome boost for morale.

Ciano wrote in his diary:

12 November
A black day. The British have attacked the Italian fleet at anchor in Taranto without warning and have sunk the dreadnought *Cavour* …

I thought I would find the Duce downhearted. Instead, he took the blow quite well and does not at the moment seem to have fully realised its gravity. When Badoglio [Marshal Pietro Badoglio Chief of the General Staff] last came to see me at the Palazzo Chigi, he said that when we attacked Greece we should immediately move the fleet, which would no longer be safe in the port of Taranto, why was this not done?[15]

Notes

1 Lamb, Charles, *War in a Stringbag* p.74
2 Ibid p.41
3 Wragg, David, *Swordfish The Story of the Taranto Raid.* p.75
4 Ciano, G. *Ciano's Diary 1937–1943* p.392
5 Bragadin, M.A. *The Italian Navy in World War II* p.42
6 Cunningham, A.B. *A Sailor's Odyssey* p.273
7 Lamb, p.104
8 Cunningham, p.285
9 Lamb, p.105
10 Arthur, Max, *Lost Voices of the Royal Navy* p.267–268
11 Wragg, p.129
12 Playfair, Major-General I.S.O. *The Mediterranean & Middle East Volume I* p.237
13 Bragadin, p.45–47
14 Cunningham, p.286
15 Ciano, p.395

7

Cape Spartivento

Days after the raid on Taranto Admiral Cunningham informed the Admiralty that with the arrival of *Barham* he could release *Ramillies*, a welcome piece of news given the activity of German raiders in the Atlantic. The cruisers *Berwick* and *Newcastle* would also return to the Home Fleet.

A plan was formed to send a fast convoy through the Mediterranean, three merchant ships, two for Malta and one for Alexandria, escorted by the 6-inch gun cruisers *Manchester* and *Southampton*, each cruiser carrying hundreds of RAF airmen, reinforcements for units in Egypt that had sent men to Greece. To the north and west Force H, *Renown*, *Ark Royal* and the cruisers *Sheffield* and *Despatch* would provide support.

Force D would sail from Alexandria, comprising the battleship *Ramillies*, cruisers *Newcastle* and *Berwick* supported by the anti-aircraft cruiser *Coventry* and five destroyers to join Force H. Meanwhile *Manchester* and *Southampton* passed to the east where *Coventry* and her destroyers would join them.

The rest of the Mediterranean Fleet was engaged in support of Greece. Aircraft from *Illustrious* attacked the seaplane base at Leros, while Eagle's aircraft attacked Tripoli. Much of the surface fleet was covering convoys south and east of Malta.

Supermarina, informed that Force H and the convoy had put to sea from Gibraltar, ordered the Italian fleet to sea on 26 November, consisting of the *Vittorio Veneto* and *Cesare* with six heavy cruisers and fourteen destroyers commanded by Admiral Campioni. The Sicilian channel was covered by torpedo boats and destroyers.

At dawn the next day Force H was about 100 miles to the south west of Cape Spartivento. The *Manchester* and *Southampton* with the merchant ships were 25 miles west-south-west. Reconnaissance from Malta had not picked up the Italian ships. Spotter aircraft from *Ark Royal* also initially found nothing until 09:00 when they raised the alarm, having spotted cruisers and destroyers south of Cape Spartivento steering southwest.

At first Admiral Somerville thought the aircraft report might have identified Force D coming from the east. By 10:15 they were confirmed as enemy ships. However Force D had been confirmed approaching from the southeast; Somerville now concentrated his ships. Within 30 minutes the two British fleets were within sight of each other.

The convoy was directed to steer well to the south inside Galita Island with destroyers and the old cruiser *Despatch*. *Ark Royal* prepared strike aircraft. The cruisers *Sheffield*, *Southampton*, *Newcastle*, *Manchester* and *Berwick* steered north toward the enemy, taking up the vanguard with five destroyers. *Ramillies* and *Renown* followed the cruisers at their best speeds. *Renown* was down to 27 knots because of a hot bearing in one shaft, but soon overtook *Ramillies* that was making her best speed of 20.7 knots.[1]

Captain A.W. Grey of *Renown*, in his official report indicated 'The temperature of the bearing continued to fluctuate.' although they ran the starboard inner shaft at slower revs 'it was essential to keep the ship in action at the highest possible speed.'[2]

About 11:15 it was reported the enemy had turned away to the east. Somerville was still unsure of what he faced but knew it was vital to remain between the enemy and the convoy and 'it was essential to show a bold front and attack the enemy as soon as possible.'[3]

Admiral Campioni, at about 10:15, received a report from a cruiser's catapult aircraft that one battleship, two cruisers and four destroyers were 135 miles southwest of Cape Spartivento steering east. They had spotted *Renown*, although she was 30 miles closer, but they had failed to spot *Ark Royal*.

Campioni turned his force to the southeast at about 11:20. He was expecting a clash with *Renown* but wanting it to take place closer to Sicily. Around noon he received another report telling him of the junction between Force H and D, and the presence of an aircraft carrier. Another inaccurate report came in stating there were three British battleships. With the critical situation of the Italian fleet after the Taranto raid, Campioni's orders were to 'Seek battle only when in decisively superior force.' Thus Campioni had the signal hoisted, 'Do not join action', and the fleet turned away to the east to return to Naples. In fact, apart from *Ark Royal*, the two sides were about equal in strength.

However the cruisers had already joined action. From *Renown* smoke had been sighted to the north at 12:15; minutes later the Italian cruisers opened fire. The British cruisers and *Renown* replied; even *Ramillies* fired two salvoes. All shots from the capital ships fell short.

On board *Renown* all knew when the main armament was firing. Stoker Petty Officer Bill Cain recalled 'I was down below during the action and the sensation of having those 15-inch guns firing was terrific. One had the sensation of standing still for a second then leaping forward again after the concussion.'[4] Leading Steward Ted Smith felt that the ship 'literally shook in such conditions and dust rose and loose cork [anti-drip-condensation] dropped from the deck-heads in great showers.'[5]

A running fight developed between the cruisers on an east-north-east course as both sides strained at their highest speeds, but the faster Italian ships began pulling away. From one of the first enemy salvoes the *Berwick*'s after turret was put out of action, and fifteen minutes later she was hit again.

At 12:44 eleven aircraft from *Ark Royal* attacked the Italian battleships; they concentrated on *Vittorio Veneto* but no hits were made and all aircraft returned safely. In the heat of battle the pilots mistakenly thought they had hit the battleships, and the anti-aircraft gunners thought some of the aircraft had been shot down.

The cruiser action continued, but no further damage was inflicted on either side. The only loss to the Italian fleet was the destroyer *Lanciere,* which was damaged and left dead in the water.

About 13:00 the British cruisers sighted the enemy battleships and soon came under a rain of heavy calibre shells. They turned away to the southeast under a smokescreen hoping the Italians would follow them toward *Renown*. However the Italians continued moving away east. The British cruisers took up the chase again, but could not close the gap and at 13:18 the action ceased.[6]

Also at 13:15 Admiral Somerville had decided to give up the chase and return to cover the convoy's movement to the east and Malta. The fleet commanders came under criticism from both their political and military masters. Admiral Somerville on the return to Gibraltar found he was to face a board of enquiry; Churchill was all for replacing him. The board sat from 3–5 December and on the 6th announced their findings. These were that the original orders for the operations by Admiral Somerville were clear and concise; that the action was conducted in a correct and spirited manner conducive to the safety of the convoy and its timely arrival at its destination in the face of a superior enemy; and that the decision to abandon the chase at 13:10, although slightly early, was the correct one.

The Admiralty grudgingly accepted the report, reminding Somerville that his main objective was to 'destroy the enemy', but Churchill had failed in his bid to have Somerville removed from command.[7] The First Sea Lord mentioned the board in a letter to Cunningham, who was quick to voice his opinion in reply.

> You ask me if I was surprised at the board of enquiry on Force H's action south of Sardinia. You will wish me to speak out quite frankly and say that I was very sorry for the decision, more especially as the board was set up before Force H had returned to harbour.
>
> The action was an unsatisfactory one. When one is burdened with a convoy one's hands are always tied to a certain extent. [This desired freedom of action from convoy responsibility would benefit Cunningham at Matapan.]
>
> At the time I thought it intolerable that a Flag officer, doing his utmost in difficult circumstances should be continuously under the threat of findings of a board of enquiry waiting for him on his return to harbour if his action failed to commend themselves to those at home who knew little or nothing of the real facts of the case.[8]

The encounter off Cape Teulada, as the Italians called the Cape Spartivento action, was far from satisfactory from their point of view as well.

The British had achieved their main aim of passing the convoy through unscathed. Again inaccurate reconnaissance had dogged Admiral Campioni leading him to the wrong conclusions. The complete lack of effective air support was another factor, leaving the fleet open to carrier born attacks, although the fleet was close to Sardinian airfields. Requests for air support had to go via Supermarina, which in turn had to forward the request to Air Force High Command, which then went back down the chain of command to the regional airfields, an antiquated system. It was hardly surprising therefore that the Regia Aeronautica usually turned up late or not at all.

The war in Greece and Albania had gone from bad to worse, sparking a crisis in the Italian High Command, as noted in Ciano's diary.

26 November
Badoglio, after a conference with the Duce, has handed in his resignation.

28 November
Bad news from Albania Greek pressure continues, but above all our resistance is weakening.

5 December
The Duce intends to replace Admiral Cavagnari with Admiral Riccardi. My father's opinion of the latter was not very high.[9]

In this reshuffle Admiral Campioni became Deputy Chief of Staff, effectively a desk job. He was replaced as fleet commander by Admiral Angelo Iachino, who had certainly shown a degree of aggression while commanding the 1st Cruiser Division.

Toward the end of 1940 it had become apparent to Admiral Cunningham that the Italian fleet now posed more of a threat in the western basin of the Mediterranean. In view of this he proposed sending the battleship *Malaya* to reinforce Force H. Once more it was done with the passage of a westbound convoy.

Warspite made her first visit to Malta in 1940 at this time. The island's population and defenders were in good heart. The air attacks, which had started with such severity in June, had dwindled to virtually nothing, although air defence on the island was still a problem. Even the dockyard was practically back to normal as regards repair work.

The naval outlook in the Mediterranean at the end of 1940 for the British was good. They had a fair degree of control throughout the sea's length, but things were about to change, as foreshadowed in Ciano's diary:

6 December:
Conference with Marshal Milch, [Field Marshal Erhard Von Milch, and Hitler's Secretary of State for Air] who has come to Rome to

settle the question of the Stukas in the Mediterranean. He was calm and optimistic about the situation in general, including the Greek Question.[10]

Notes

1 Ciano, G. *Ciano's Diary 1937–1943* p.395
2 Playfair, Major-General I.S.O. *The Mediterranean & Middle East Volume I* p.302
3 Smith, Peter C. *Hit First Hit Hard:* HMS *Renown 1916–1948* p.157
4 Ibid p.159
5 Ibid p.165
6 Playfair, p.305
7 Ibid p.306–307
8 Cunningham, A.B. *A Sailor's Odyssey* p.293–294
9 Ciano, p.399–401
10 Ibid p402

8

Enter the Luftwaffe

A letter from Adolf Hitler to Mussolini on 20 November 1940 was largely a lecture on the deplorable consequences of Italy's premature action against Greece. Mussolini was heard to comment on reading it: 'He has really smacked my fingers.' In the letter the Führer continued his proposal made to Count Ciano on his visit to the Berghof a few days before, part of which was to transfer German air units to Italy.[1]

On 10 December orders were issued for Fliegerkorps X from Norway – a unit that had specialised in attacks on shipping – to move to airfields in southern Italy. By 8 January, 96 bombers were established on Sicilian airfields; by mid-January the figure had risen to 186 aircraft of all types. The best aircraft for ship attacks was the JU 87 Stuka dive-bomber.

The Luftwaffe had ostensibly come to support the Regia Aeronautica but was soon calling the shots. The first priority was to attack British shipping, with the carrier *Illustrious* high on the list of targets. Next was to neutralise Malta. Later the mining of the Suez Canal and Alexandria was a consideration but this would really need the occupation of Crete, as most Luftwaffe aircraft were short range.

On 8 January the Regia Marina was bombed by Malta-based RAF Wellingtons at Naples. They managed to damage the *Cesare*, which resulted in Supermarina moving the capital ships further north.[2]

On 10 January the entire Mediterranean Fleet was at sea to take over escorting the eastbound convoy from Gibraltar, Operation *Excess*. Force H would cover the convoy as far as Sicily and then Cunningham would take over. Italian Savoia-Marchetti SM79s bombed the convoy with no success and lost two aircraft to *Ark Royal*'s Fulmars.

Charles Lamb on *Illustrious* recalled relaxing that fateful day in the early morning sunshine; he was gazing astern watching the destroyer HMS *Gallant* trying to catch up to her station on the carrier's port quarter having carried out another task at full speed.

'As we stood looking at the destroyer she broke into two pieces and the focsle sank at once, leaving the bulk of the ship wallowing on the surface like an open-ended tin box.'

This was quickly followed by the sound of the explosion. *Gallant* had hit a mine. What remained of the destroyer was towed into Malta, though she was never repaired.[3]

There was a certain amount of discontent on board *Illustrious* at the time over whether the carrier should have been taken so close into danger. Admiral Lyster and the ship's Captain Denis Boyd pointed out to Cunningham that 806 Squadron only had a handful of serviceable fighter aircraft, and the carrier could still supply a degree of cover while out of range of enemy aircraft.

Cunningham replied that *Illustrious* was 'to remain on station.'[4] However it would have been difficult to supply an escort for the carrier alone. As usual Cunningham was short of destroyers; he had seven with the fleet, then six with the loss of *Gallant*.

The Stukas and JU 88s soon found the fleet and concentrated on *Illustrious* which flew off more fighters to join what she had in the air. 'At times she became almost completely hidden in a forest of great splashes', wrote Cunningham as the enemy attacked *Illustrious*,

I saw her hit early on just before the bridge, and in all, in something like ten minutes, she was hit by six 1,000lb bombs, to leave the line badly on fire, her steering gear crippled, her lifts out of action, and with heavy casualties.[5]

Stoker Albert Jones of *Illustrious*:

Things then began to happen so fast and changed to near chaos as the Germans began to score hits on us. With each successive explosion and the gunfire up top, a horrendous cacophony could be heard.

The second attack brought more hits.

Suddenly there was a tremendous explosion and the ship shuddered from stem to stern under the impact as if some unknown force had struck us with a gigantic sledgehammer.[6]

By 13:30 *Illustrious* was severely damaged. Bombs had wrecked the flight deck twisting it into grotesque shapes, destroyed nine aircraft, put half her guns out of action, and set the ship on fire fore and aft. Captain Boyd was ordered to make for Malta. For three hours the crew struggled to regain control; her steering gear had been disabled and she turned in circles. Control was finally regained by using the main engines to steer. About 16:00 she was attacked again but only hit once.

An hour later the battleships were attacked by fourteen aircraft but no hits were made. In an earlier attack *Warspite* had been hit once but the bomb had burst against the starboard bower anchor causing no great damage. On *Valiant* one man was killed and two wounded by splinters from a near miss. The enemy were chased off by Fulmars from *Illustrious* which had landed on Malta; refuelled and rearmed they had returned to aid the fleet.

By this time *Illustrious* was close to the southern shore of Malta. The fleet remained close at hand trying to lend her anti-aircraft fire support, but they parted company about 17:30. Finally, an hour after sunset with the stricken carrier five miles from the entrance to Valletta harbour, she was attacked by torpedo bombers. They were driven off by gunfire and at about 21:00 *Illustrious* limped into Valletta. Her crew had suffered 126 killed and 91 wounded.

With *Illustrious* seriously damaged and seemingly trapped at Malta, although if she managed to get away she would require months in a dockyard, the fleet had lost its vital air support. The Admiralty acted speedily on 12 January – before the Mediterranean Fleet had even arrived back in Alexandria – by ordering the carrier *Formidable*, which had been due to replace *Ark Royal* in Force H, to join Cunningham's fleet instead. She was seen as so valuable that her passage to Alexandria would be via the long Cape route. When *Formidable* arrived the old *Eagle* would leave the fleet for major repairs.

The cruisers *Gloucester* and *Southampton* were sent to support the east-bound convoy M.E.6. At 12:00 on 11 January they were about 30 miles astern of the convoy when they were attacked by a dozen dive bombers; neither ship was fitted with radar so they were taken by surprise. Two or three bombs hit *Southampton* causing serious damage. One hit was made on *Gloucester* but the bomb penetrated five decks without exploding. For an hour the crew struggled to save the ship, but loss of water for her boilers brought her to a stop at 16:40. Fires on board could not be brought under control so at 22:00 the order was given to abandon ship; 80 of her crew had been killed and 87 wounded. The light cruiser *Orion* sank her with three torpedos.[7]

RAF Wellingtons from Malta hit the Luftwaffe airfields at Catania in Sicily on the night of 12 January. Buildings were hit and some 30 aircraft were destroyed on the ground. However they were unable to stem the rising tide as more German aircraft arrived. On 16 January the first attacks by the Fliegerkorps X began on the harbours of Malta and on *Illustrious*, as her crew and the dockyard workers struggled to make her ready for sea. The dockyard was damaged and there were some 100 civilian casualties. *Illustrious* was hit again but suffered only minor damage.

After this raid it was decided to move most of the carrier's crew ashore leaving only a skeleton crew on board while the engineers worked around the clock to repair the steering gear. Even the ship's anti-aircraft gunners went ashore as half their guns were out of action. Anti-aircraft defence was left to the army's batteries around the harbour, augmented by the old monitor, *Terror*, and the Australian cruiser *Perth*, however the latter was badly damaged by a near miss.

Joseph Caruana watched the plight of *Illustrious*.

> The aircraft carrier was across the creek from Senglea, and my town was well within the target area. The noise and commotion was fantastic and my memories are a kaleidoscope of terror. The whining war cry of the diving Stukas, the loud and incessant firing of the AA guns; the terrifying shaking of the ground and house with each bomb explosion ... After the raid I remember people staring, dazed and awed, at the destruction while others worked with frantic haste to rescue people buried under the demolished houses ... while that area of the town abreast the moorings of *Illustrious* was pulverised into a carpet of rubble. *Illustrious* was still afloat and apparently undamaged.[8]

Kathleen Norman, a naval wife, recorded the scenes around and on board *Illustrious*.

Each day, as we came in at the gate, there was some fresh scene of
devastation. Workshops lay piled in rubble and glass. Iron girders were
twisted and torn … [The crew] had lost most of their gear. They were
dressed in old boiler overalls, in grey flannel trousers and sweaters any
old garment they had managed to rescue from the wrecks of their
cabins. The surgeon of the ship had done wonderful work in the battle
at sea. He was pale, and his face was very, very, sad.

Surgeon Commander Keevil was awarded the DSO for his work on
Illustrious and ashore on Malta. Mrs Norman went on board the battered
carrier.

It was the first time I had ever been on board a wounded ship. When
I saw *Illustrious's* great torn decks, the aching chasm that reached into
her bowels, the little sickbay that had known such horror, I felt almost
as near tears as when I talked with her tired seamen.[9]

Three days later the attack was renewed by swarms of Stukas and fighters.
They concentrated on Malta's airfields at Hal Far and Luqa; six aircraft
were destroyed on the ground and many damaged. *Illustrious* it was hoped
would sail on the 20th but heavy attacks on the 19th in the dockyard
areas resulted in underwater damage to her keel plating, requiring further
repairs. Finally the Vice-Admiral Malta, Sir Wilbraham Ford was able to
report the carrier ready for sea on the evening of the 23rd.

At dusk that day *Illustrious* crept out of harbour unobserved by the
enemy. At Suda Bay destroyers and cruisers had been assembled to cover
her passage. Two merchant ships left just before her to take advantage
of this cover as well. That night she ran up to 24 knots. The cruisers
and destroyers missed her, not expecting such a turn of speed from the
patched up vessel. They came under attack by enemy aircraft but suffered
no heavy damage. *Illustrious* escaped unscathed, on this occasion, helped
by poor visibility. At noon on the 25th *Illustrious* steamed into Alexandria
harbour, to be cheered by every ship there. Admiral Cunningham noted:

That *Illustrious* episode stands out as a triumph for British shipbuild-
ing and our naval constructors, as well as for those who repaired her
at Malta. I sent a message to the Vice-Admiral at Malta expressing our
warmest appreciation of the work done under conditions of great dif-

ficulty to get the ship away. The men of Malta dockyard deserved all
the praise we could give them.[10]

Illustrious was soon on her way again on her journey to the US, where
she would be extensively rebuilt at Norfolk in Virginia. *Formidable* would
join the fleet in March.

The arrival of the Fliegerkorps in the central Mediterranean completely changed the military situation, making the use of shipping in
daylight within the range of the dive bombers extremely expensive
in terms of men and ships. Convoys for Alexandria were now routed
around the Cape. To restore freedom of movement would require more
fighters, both carrier-borne and shore-based, and more bombers, but
aircraft of all types were in short supply.

Meanwhile the importance of Malta as a base had become greater
than ever. Airfields in the bulge of Cyrenacia were being secured, which
would bring a degree of air cover to the central Mediterranean and support for Malta. The island's role as an offensive base was paramount. RAF
Wellingtons kept up their attacks against Sicilian airfields when they
could. While Navy Swordfish based on Malta continued to attack Axis
shipping, five submarines of the small 'U' class were based on the island
and, with other larger longer range boats, were also taking an increasing
toll on enemy shipping.

Since the raid on Taranto and the redeployment of the Italian fleet to
the west coast ports of Italy, Admiral Somerville had considered attacking
these ports from the sea. Intelligence suggested that one of the *Vittorio
Veneto* class battleships was under repair in Genoa. The port that could be
bombarded from the sea, in waters that were too deep to be mined, but
Genoa was 700 miles from the base of Force H, right in the backyard of the
enemy. It was possible there might not even be any Italian heavy naval units
there, but the effect on morale of striking the enemy so far north could
be considerable. Cunningham agreed to Somerville's plan. The Admiralty
suggested a subsidiary operation to attack the Tirso dam in Sardinia with
torpedo aircraft; the dam supplied much of the island's power.[11]

On 23 January the information was that *Littorio* was in dry dock and
Giulio Cesare was alongside at Genoa. A long range photographic Spitfire
was sent to confirm this from Malta but was shot down.

On the evening of 31 January Force H – *Renown, Malaya, Ark Royal,
Sheffield* and ten destroyers – sailed from Gibraltar. The plan was to attack

the Tirso dam on 2 February and bombard Genoa the next day, while Admiral Cunningham sailed westward from Alexandria with part of his fleet to create a diversion.

Eight aircraft of No 810 Squadron carrying torpedoes were flown from *Ark Royal* at 06:00 into deteriorating weather. They were met by heavy anti-aircraft fire over the targets; no hits were seen on the dam, and the Air Ministry had warned torpedoes would be unsuitable. One aircraft was lost.

The weather rapidly worsened, developing into a gale from the northeast slowing the speed of Force H. This would have meant an approach to Genoa in daylight so the operation was abandoned.

On 6 February Force H sailed again in two groups trying to confuse the enemy. The whole force concentrated early on the 8th north of Majorca. At 04:00 after a calm if moonlit passage, *Ark Royal* was detached with a destroyer escort to bomb the oil refinery at Leghorn and lay mines off Spezia. Two hours later catapult aircraft were launched from the bombardment group to spot the fall of shot. At 07:11 *Renown's* aircraft reported that no battleships could be seen. This was an error as *Duilio* was in fact in dry dock.

The sea was calm; there was no sign of shipping and the sky was clear of enemy aircraft. The gulf of Genoa was covered in sea fog but the spotting aircraft had a bird's eye view. At 07:15 the battleships opened fire. Force H fired some 300 tons of shells into Genoa, 273 rounds of 15-inch, 782 rounds of 6-inch and 400 rounds of 4.5-inch. Many merchant ships in the harbour were damaged, but *Duilio* escaped unscathed. CPO Charles Wright had mixed emotions about the bombardment;

> What a delightful place this was in peacetime when I was in *Resolution*. How different in war. I remember being on *Renown's* boat deck watching the destruction of the wharves and the Ansaldo works, when a voice behind me said, 'What are you doing up here?' My reply was to the effect, I was in Genoa in peacetime, sir, and made many friends. The Commander's reply left me in no doubts. 'Get below. This is war.'

Admiral Somerville himself had some pangs of conscience.

> For half an hour we blazed away, and I had to think of Valletta, London, Bristol, etc, to harden my heart. But I was watching the map and the

reports of the aircraft and I do believe practically all our shots fell on works, warehouses, shipping, docks etc. Still it's no use pretending that some innocent people were not killed. War is lousy.[12]

Force H was spotted by the Italians early in the morning of the 8th. Supermarina ordered the battleships *Vittorio Veneto*, *Cesare*, and *Doria* to sail from Spezia and the heavy cruisers *Trieste*, *Trento*, and *Bolzano* from Messina to meet at dawn on 9 February 40 miles west of the Boniface strait, between Corsica and Sardinia. According to Commander Bragadin in the official history, this was 'much further north than the standing orders for this type of situation which called for a rendezvous southwest of Sardinia.'[13]

This meant Admiral Iachino's force was at sea before *Ark Royal's* aircraft had mined the approaches to Spezia. His fleet was well placed to intercept Force H on the return to Gibraltar. However a familiar sequence of events began to unfold; Italian reconnaissance and inter-service cooperation was poor. Iachino received conflicting reports and his own fleet's catapult aircraft found nothing. Regia Aeronautica aircraft did find Force H more than once, some even attacked it but scored no hits, but this information was not integrated into the Italian air-sea com-munications system. Thus Supermarina only received the reports once the aircraft had returned to base. As Commander Bragadin summed up; 'it must be said that the day, which for a great many reasons had begun with such favourable prospects, ended in deep disappointment.'[14]

It was remarkable that a British fleet, that must have expected to be spotted, had attacked a port in the north of Italy inflicting damage and had escaped unscathed without even coming under serious attack, all this against the combined might of the Regia Marina, Regia Aeronautica and the Luftwaffe. It demonstrated the arrival of German air power had not secured control of the Mediterranean for the Axis, and all eyes now turned toward Greece.

Notes
1 Bullock, Alan, *Hitler a Study in Tyranny* p.573
2 Playfair, Major-General I.S.O. *The Mediterranean & Middle East Volume I* p.315
3 Lamb, Charles, *War in a Stringbag* p.121–122
4 Ibid p.123
5 Cunningham A.B. *A Sailor's Odyssey* p.302–303
6 Wragg, David, *Swordfish* p.152

7 Playfair, p.320

8 Elliot, Peter, *The Cross and the Ensign. A Naval History of Malta 1798–1979* p.126

9 Perowne, Stewart, *The Siege within the Walls: Malta 1940–1943* p.68

10 Cunningham, p.305

11 Playfair, p.329

12 Smith, Peter C. *Hit First Hit Hard: HMS Renown 1916–1948* p.183

13 Bragadin, M.A. *The Italian Navy in World War II* p.65

14 Ibid p66

PART TWO

Matapan

Coming from the west one often makes a landfall at Cape Matapan, the low-lying point where the tall Taygetos range of the Mani penin-sula falls insignificantly into the sea. The cape is so low that one can often see the lighthouse before the point of land.

H.M. Denham[1]

9

Reluctant Allies

In February 1941, at Merano in the foothills of the Dolomite Mountains, the Chief of Staff of the Regia Marina, Admiral Arturo Riccardi, and his German counterpart, Admiral Erich Raeder, along with their staffs, met for three days. This was ostensibly to exchange ideas and experiences, for up to that time the Axis partners had largely been fighting their own wars keeping their plans broadly hidden from each other.

However Italian war aims had largely failed. The short war theory lay in tatters. More and more Italy would have to rely on her northern ally for supplies and materials merely to keep her in the war. A war that was becoming increasingly unpopular with the Italian public.

The Germans were not merely going to supply their erratic ally; rather, fully equipped German units like Fliegerkorps X of the Luftwaffe, and the Africa Korps which began arriving in the early days of February, would take up the fight. The aim of this involvement in the Mediterranean would result in the war being directed from Berlin. The Italians could not continue without material aid so had to accept German domination.

This situation for the Italian armed forces fell hardest on the navy, who felt it bordered on the absurd, as Germany was not even an important naval power. But they did come to an understanding over German action in Greece, and the Italians hoped to resolve the growing problems of fuel supplies, which had become dire. The Regia Marina had begun the war with 1,800,000 tons of fuel but by the time of the Merano meeting 1,000,000 tons had been used. According to Commander Bragadin:

At this rate, the Italian fleet would have to cease all activity by the coming summer. This tremendously grave problem naturally had already been brought to the attention of the supreme command many times, but nothing of a reassuring nature had been agreed upon with Germany. For this reason it was hoped that direct conversations with German Navy chiefs, who were professional people more capable of understanding such problems, would bring about a satisfactory solution of the problem.[2]

The involvement of Admiral Raeder in the Italian naval fuel supplies did ease the situation. By the spring of 1941 more regular deliveries were arriving, however even then it was about 50,000 tons a month, only a quarter of what was required. Indeed by the summer of 1941 the navy ran out of fuel and was paralysed.

However the main German concern of the conference was the imminent German invasion of Greece which they felt would be heavily reinforced by the British. They felt the Italian fleet should be able to carry out offensive sweeps against the British line of supply from Egypt to Greece. Admiral Riccardi pointed out this would be difficult to achieve because of the proved effectiveness of British air reconnaissance, and the distance from the fleet's bases would put any convoys quickly beyond their reach. 'The Germans appeared to be convinced by the Admiral's explanation, and the subject was dropped.'[3]

However at the beginning of March, Berlin informed Rome of the nearness of their intervention in Greece and the Balkans, and they expected the Italians to do their utmost to block British aid to Greece. German commanders had voiced cynical contempt of their ally's navy; Field Marshal Kesselring was one.

The Italian Navy was regarded as a piece de resistance and was therefore used sparingly-an attitude which caused special internal difficulties. Yet three times we managed to overcome these and get it to put to sea. A further trouble lay in its being stationed in different harbours; to assemble it cost time and wasted fuel. Finally, one or other battleship was either not ready to put to sea, or was not fuelled, or was in dock. Exercises in large formations could not be carried out mainly because of this same shortage of fuel. Gunnery practice was a rarity. On top of this there were extraordinary technical deficiencies which deservedly earned the Italian navy the nickname 'Fair–weather Fleet.' Its doubtful seaworthiness called for increased air protection and that, with the limited strength of the Axis air forces in the Mediterranean, imposed ridiculous demands on the German Luftwaffe, whose hands were already full protecting convoys. If the Italian fleet by any chance ever came within extreme range of the British fleets and a few shots were actually exchanged, it had to break off the engagement at the approach of dusk because of its inability to fire in the dark, and run for the nearest port Taranto or Messina.[4]

Kesselring had a point, but his views are pretty typical of land-based commanders with little naval experience.

Having been ordered by the Italian High Command to intervene in the British build up, Supermarina ordered more submarines into Cretan waters, a special assault team was ordered to strike against ships in Suda Bay, and heavy surface units were ordered to carry out offensive sweeps. 'Supermarina undertook this reluctantly feeling that the risks that they entailed were far greater than the very unlikely probability of surprising an enemy convoy in Cretan Waters.'[5]

The Germans promised closer cooperation with Fliegerkorps X, the latter having claimed they had hit two of the three British battleships from the Mediterranean Fleet west of Crete on 16 March. Supermarina was also assured they would have greater air reconnaissance by the Luftwaffe over Alexandria and the central Mediterranean. They would increase bombing raids on Malta, and fighter sweeps to intercept British spotter aircraft from the island. When the fleet was at sea aircraft from the Regia Aeronautica would bomb British airfields on Crete and carry out reconnaissance of the British supply routes north from Alexandria. Also fighter aircraft from Rhodes would cover the ships in the Crete area. A great many promises were made by the airmen.

On 19 March the German Naval Liaison Officer in Rome handed the following communication to the Italian Naval Staff.

Subject: Naval Strategic situation in the Mediterranean.

The German Naval Staff has instructed me to communicate to you the following views of the Commander-in-Chief of the German Navy.

The German Naval Staff considers that at the moment there is only one British Battleship [*Valiant*] fully ready for action in the east Mediterranean. It is not anticipated that the British will withdraw heavy units from the Atlantic in the near future. Force H is also considered unlikely to appear in the eastern Mediterranean. Thus, the situation in the East Mediterranean is more favourable for the Italian fleet at this moment than ever before. The intensive traffic from Alexandria to the Greek ports, by which the Greek forces are receiving constant reinforcements both in men and equipment, presents a particularly worthwhile target for the Italian naval forces.

The German Naval Staff considers that the appearance of Italian units in the area south of Crete will seriously interfere with British shipping, and may even lead to the complete interruption of the transport of troops, especially as these transports are at the moment inadequately protected.[6]

This communication was based on Fliegerkorps X's claim to have damaged two British battleships on 16 March.

Of course this could have been fairly easily checked out on the ground. They had time a week before the fleet sailed and there were many Axis agents in Alexandria. John Eppler – known as 'Rommel's Spy' – whenever he was in the port, always viewed the harbour, later sketching what he saw and reporting to his masters.[7]

The Germans also seemed unaware that on 10 March the armoured aircraft carrier *Formidable* had reached Alexandria via the Suez Canal. It was as if the Germans and Italians were guilty of listening to only the intelligence they wanted to hear.

Admiral Angelo Iachino was 52 in 1941. He had joined the navy in 1904 at the academy at Livorno, graduating in 1907. He commanded a torpedo boat during the First World War, and was naval attaché to the Italian embassy in China 1923–1928. He had been promoted Admiral a few months before Italy entered the Second World War.

Iachino had an upright bearing, with a trim figure of middle height; his steely blue eyes gazed out beneath a high forehead giving him a brooding appearance, which was not his nature. A man of few words who was known for his affable temperament, he had the ability, envied by many officers, to make commands clear to his subordinates. He was held in high regard by all those who ever served with him.

Since Iachino had taken command of the Italian surface fleet he had been itching to get at the enemy. He was well aware of increased British convoys to Greece from Egyptian ports and felt something should and could be done in the eastern Mediterranean, but only by the faster modern Italian ships. His older slower battleships were unsuitable for the hit–and–run tactics he had in mind. At that time only the *Vittorio Veneto* was ready for sea, in his plan to be accompanied by numerous cruisers and destroyers.

He wrote an outline of the operation, typing it up himself, and at the end of February sent it to the Naval Chief of Staff Admiral Riccardi, who quickly replied stating the High Command had been thinking along similar lines, and certainly intended to implement such action when the battle fleet returned to Taranto once the harbour defences there were improved.

He felt certain changes would affect the plan; the British were no longer using Benghazi for convoys to Greece, restricting themselves to Tobruk and the Egyptian ports. This would mean the focus of the operation would be further east, but the fleet was still operating under strict fuel economy.

However after the German communication of 19 March, Iachino was summoned to Supermarina at Rome for a meeting with the Chief-of-Staff, when he was told his plan was to be implemented, with some variation. The plan consisted of two offensive sweeps to be carried out simultaneously, one south of the small island of Gavdos 30 miles southwest of Crete; the other north of Crete into the western Aegean, areas where Luftwaffe reconnaissance aircraft were reporting daily that British convoys were operating. Secrecy was vital, particularly in the Italian ports where there were many British agents and sympathisers. The execution order from Rome to the various fleet commanders would be sent by telegram.

Vittorio Veneto was moved from La Spezia to Naples on 22 March. The operation was scheduled for 24 March, but the date was postponed for two days at the request of the Luftwaffe.

The Germans wished to come to direct agreement with Admiral Iachino in determining the details of their air assistance, since on this occasion X Cat [German air command in the Mediterranean] was collaborating with the Italian Navy for the first time. Among the things decided was that X Cat would carry out an escort and ship identification exercise with a large number of aircraft on the day that the Italian naval forces passed out of the straits of Messina.[8]

On 25 March two German officers from Fliegerkorps X arrived aboard *Vittorio Veneto*, Captain Withus and Lieutenant Maser along with Lieutenant Colussi, the liaison officer between the Regia Marina and the Luftwaffe in Sicily. Although they had little time, a rudimentary plan was worked out for cooperation at sea between Fliegerkorps X and the Italian navy. Maser and Colussi, it was decided, would remain on board with a German radio operator throughout the operation. That night a courier from Rome arrived on the flagship; he carried documents detailing the agreements between Supermarina and the two air forces which provided for reconnaissance over Alexandria and Suda Bay and the areas south of the toe of Italy and east of Sicily, plus the fighter sweeps and bomber raids against Malta and attacks on British bases on Crete.

Admiral Iachino went over these plans in fine detail with his air liaison officer, Major Fantana, who soon gave in his opinion that the aircraft would be unable to supply the fleet with adequate air cover, mainly for the reason the aircraft involved simply did not have the range or endurance. Iachino telephoned Supermarina, informing Admiral Campioni, Vice Chief of the Naval Staff, that the air cover he insisted on was in some doubt. Campioni was in no mood to go through it all again, but finally reluctantly agreed to do so. This still did not satisfy Iachino who went to the Chief of Staff Admiral Riccardi, who promised him if the air cover was not up to scratch the operation would be cancelled.

Iachino put his doubts in a letter to Riccardi, worrying that the various high commands would continue arguing after he had sailed, but he held off sending it while waiting for a telephone call from Campioni which came through minutes before sailing and was still vague. He was to regret not sending the letter.

Vittorio Veneto slipped her moorings from the buoys near the San Vincenzo mole on the evening of 26 March. She had been moored there behind heavy torpedo nets and away from prying Neapolitan eyes. She fell in line behind her four escorting destroyers taking the southerly channel, kept swept of mines, between Point Campanella and the Isle of Capri. The 1st Division consisting of the heavy cruisers *Zara*, *Pola* and *Fiume* with four destroyers sailed from Taranto under the command of Admiral Cattaneo. From Brindisi came Admiral Legnani with the 8th Division with the light cruisers *Abruzzi* and *Garibaldi* and two destroyers. At dawn on the 27th *Vittorio Veneto* passed through the straits of

Messina where she was led by the 3rd Division which had left Messina shortly before, consisting of the heavy cruisers *Trieste, Trento, Bolzano* and three destroyers under the command of Admiral Sansonetti. By 11:00 all groups had joined the flagship.

From this moment the fleet would sail southeast toward Apollonia (Cyrenaica) until 20:00. By that time, being off the west coast of Crete, the 1st and 8th Divisions were to push into the Aegean Sea as far as the extreme eastern longitude of Crete, which they expected to reach about 08:00 on 28 March. From there they were to reverse course rejoining the rest of the fleet at about 15:00, 90 miles south of Navarino. *Vittorio Veneto* and the 3rd Division were to sail south of Crete to a point near the island of Gavdos at about 07:00; if no contact was made they would reverse their course.[9]

As the Italian fleet moved down the straits of Messina, a Sirocco wind began to blow, unusual at that time of the year. The sea became choppy, the wind rising to a force 4, accompanied by a mist reducing visibility to 5,000 yards.

Admiral Iachino welcomed the weather; it would aid concealment and operational surprise, providing it did not deteriorate much further and affect the speed of the destroyers. However the weather giving one advantage took away another: the German aircraft did not turn up for the agreed combined exercises because of poor visibility. Even in the afternoon when the mist partially cleared, only a few aircraft from the Luftwaffe were sighted.

The clearing mist brought another problem when at 12:20 the *Trieste* reported a British Sunderland reconnaissance aircraft which circled for about half an hour in the distance and then disappeared. The poor visibility meant the Sunderland crew only sighted the 3rd Division, as was learned from its radio reports decoded by cipher experts on the flagship. They had not spotted *Vittorio Veneto* and the other cruisers which were following further back. However, 'the sighting eliminated the first prerequisite of the operation, surprise.'[10]

Admiral Iachino must have been disheartened by this turn of events. Even his change of course to the south to try and fool the watching aircraft went unreported. He was sure Admiral Cunningham would now know the Regia Marina was at sea, and this was to his disadvantage. Unknown to Iachino, or anybody on the Italian side, Cunningham had been aware of the Italian plans for days.

Notes

1 Denham, H.M. *The Aegean* p.3
2 Bragadin, M.A. *The Italian Navy in World War II* p.81–82
3 Ibid p83
4 Kesselring, A. *The Memories of Field Marshal Kesselring*
5 Bragadin, p.84
6 Seth, Ronald, *Two Fleets Surprised: The Battle of Matapan* p.20
7 Eppler, John, *Operation Condor: Rommel's Spy* p.141
8 Bragadin, p.84–85
9 Ibid p.85
10 Ibid p.86

10

Hut 8

No warning came from enigma or any other source of the raid by Italian explosive motor boats in Suda Bay on 26 March. Once again Italian Special Forces managed to maintain secrecy.[1]

In the early morning Suda Bay was attacked by six explosive motor boats. The heavy cruiser *York* was badly damaged, her boiler and engine rooms flooded; in an effort to save her she was beached. A grave loss at the time as she was the centre of communications between the fleet and Fleet Air Arm units based on Crete. Able Seaman Christopher Buist was on board at the time:

> I was below decks when we heard these engines revving outside in the bay. We fuelled from the oiler and there was this thump followed by a mighty bang and a flash of flame right through the mess deck. The ship lifted up in the air, then down with a crash, all the lights and power went dead and it was black as hell. We went up on the fo'c'sle where all the rest of the ship's company were assembling. The ship was pulled onto the beach bows-on. As the quarterdeck was under water we lost all our stores, rum etc. We were real chokka, I can tell you.[2]

The tanker *Pericles* was also hit and holed, though the bulk of her cargo was saved. Admiral Cunningham wrote of the attack:

> Our only 8-inch gun cruiser was out of action. Once more we had paid the penalty for the inadequate defence of a fleet base.

Six prisoners were picked up on rafts, and it seemed that the explosive motor boats were sent off from two torpedo boats, and that the boats were abandoned by their crews before reaching the target. While the Italians on the whole displayed little enterprise and initiative at sea, it always amazed me how good they were at these sort of individual attacks. They certainly had men capable of the most gallant exploits.[3]

The beached *York* became a frequent target for air attacks; attempts to salvage the cruiser were abandoned in May.[4] The shipless Able Seaman Buist went on to fight with the British Army during the German invasion of Crete. He walked over the mountains to the south coast to escape capture. From there he went in a Greek caique to Egypt from which he was picked up by a British destroyer when the caique ran out of fuel and drifted.[5]

By 24/25 March Cunningham was aware from intelligence reports with some certainty that the Italian fleet would put to sea for operations in the eastern Mediterranean. It was Luftwaffe Enigma communications that first raised suspicions that the Axis forces were planning something in the central-eastern Mediterranean.

At first a landing on the Libyan coast seemed likely, but on 25 March Fliegerkorps X's Enigma revealed to the British that all twin-engine fighters from Libya were ordered to move to Palermo 'for special operations.' An Italian naval Enigma message was decoded the same day mentioning 'd minus 3' for an operation involving the Rhodes command. Another reason alarm bells were ringing loud was that the Regia Marina rarely used the Enigma code system. On 26 March further messages indicated that the targets to be attacked were airfields in the Aegean area, and there were requests for further information about British convoy movements between Alexandria and Greece, and that all this message traffic referred to the same operation.[6]

Admiral Cunningham held out the bait to the Axis for as long as he could by keeping the Lustre convoys to Piraeus and Suda Bay running. Then on the eve of the operation, the evening of the 26th, when *Vittorio Veneto* was leaving Naples, he made a series of concise signals, 'for the most part precise but giving scope for independent action. As his Flag Lieutenant at the time, Captain Hugh Lee has observed, Cunningham possessed a first rate operational mind.'[7]

Cunningham cancelled a southbound convoy from Piraeus. A convoy heading for Piraeus was to reverse course only after dark, to avoid arousing suspicion and he ordered a cruiser force to be south of Crete at dawn on 28 March. Also a Sunderland flying boat was ordered to reveal itself to the Italians so as to protect the Ultra sources.

In May 1940 Mavis Lever, at the age of nineteen, interrupted her German degree course at University College London to join the staff at the wartime deciphering centre at Bletchley Park. She was allocated to the team led by Dillwyn Knox and tasked with breaking the Italian naval Enigma code. Knox was a brilliant classical scholar, papyrologist and cryptographer who in 1917 succeeded in breaking much of the German naval code. He would break the Abwehr Enigma before dying of stomach cancer in 1943. Mavis Lever wrote of her time at Bletchley Park:

> the administration had settled in the mansion and they established their quarters in the cottage in the stable yard. Alan Turing, Gordon Welchman and John Jefferies were recruited and contact was resumed with the Polish mathematicians who had escaped to Paris from now occupied Poland.

Hut 6 became the army and air force code site, Hut 3 processed intelligence, while Hut 8 became the naval Enigma decoding site. Mavis arrived in May 1940.

> In June Mussolini joined the war and it was imperative to find out which of the Enigma machines he would be using; fortunately for their Naval High Command, or Supermarina as we soon found out it was called, it proved to be a machine without a plugboard, used by the Italian Navy in the Spanish Civil War-for which Dilly had already worked out his theoretical rodding solution.[8]

On 25 March 1941 Mavis read the encoded Supermarina message which referred to 'Today is X-3' referring to 'Operation *Gaudo*'. The team worked day and night on the flow of messages.

> Each of the three days had a different setting, of course, and each message had to be broken separately. This was the Cottage triumph of the Battle of Matapan.
> Dilly was ready with a poem to celebrate the occasion. Each verse began. 'When Cunningham won at Matapan by the grace of God and ... mentioning all his girls with a rhyming tribute, the rhyme for

Mavis conveniently began with the flattering 'rara avis.' All very heady stuff for a nineteen-year-old.[9]

Mavis met her future husband Keith Batey while working at Bletchley Park, who had been seconded from Cambridge for his technical approach. For a brief period Keith served in the Fleet Air Arm but with Knox terminally ill he was recalled to Bletchley Park. In August 1943 he solved the Enigma ciphers of the *Sicherheitsdienst*, the Nazi Party's own intelligence service, and later broke the cipher used by the Spanish military attaches in Berlin and Rome to report back to Madrid on German and Italian military plans and assessments, often working beside his wife. Keith Batey passed away during the writing of this book.

Mavis was a linguist looking for human elements and word patterns. 'It is just like driving a car' she said. 'We can both do it, but Keith understands what goes on under the bonnet.'[10, 11]

Notes

1 Hinsley, F.H. *British Intelligence in the Second World War* p.404
2 Poolman, Kenneth, *Experiences of War: The British Sailor* p.127
3 Cunningham, A.B. *A Sailor's Odyssey* p.323
4 Hinsley, p.404
5 Poolman, p.128
6 *The Cunningham Papers Vol.1: The Mediterranean Fleet 1939–1942* p.236–237
7 Erskine Ralph & Michael Smith, *Action this Day* p.100
8 Ibid p.103
9 Ibid p.105–106
10 *Daily Telegraph*. 4/10/2001
11 Ibid 5/6/2004

11

The British Fleet at Alexandria

On 23 March the Eastern Mediterranean Fleet had covered a success-
ful convoy through to beleaguered Malta, the first since January. By 24
March it was back in Alexandria harbour. The fleet had its hands full at
this time with moving the army to Greece – Operation *Lustre* – which
had begun on 4 March. However Malta had an even higher priority.
Therefore much of the fleet was used to cover the convoy of four merchant ships, three from Haifa and one from Alexandria carrying coal,
cement and a mixed cargo of foodstuffs. The convoy was routed to pass
close to the south coast of Crete so the Fleet Air Arm could provide
fighter support from Maleme. The convoy avoided air attack thanks to
low cloud and this routing. The merchant ships were damaged while
alongside in Malta but most supplies were unloaded safely.

On 24 March Surgeon Commander E.R. Sorley of the *Barham*, who
had been with the ship for a year, wrote home.

I hope you haven't been listening to the Rome Radio broadcasts.
You remember that in my last letter I said something about a spot of
excitement from which we emerged quite unscathed. It seems that
I can now reveal that this was an attack by torpedo bombers at dusk,
and we did not think much about it until Rome announced trium-
phantly that it was definitely known that the *Barham* had been hit by
two torpedoes. Take it from me, this, like most of the Axis claims is
complete 'baloney.'[1]

Malta's striking forces had been unable to prevent advanced elements of Erwin Rommel's Afrika Korps reaching Tripoli. By the end of March, 25,000 men with 8,500 vehicles were ashore.[2]

Andrew Browne Cunningham, commander of the Mediterranean Fleet, was 58 in 1941, born in Dublin of Scottish parents in January 1883. He joined the Royal Navy aged fourteen at the training ship HMS *Britannia* moored at Dartmouth. He was slim, even slight, with a thin angular face quick to show humour, although his blue eyes revealed iron determination. His voice was seldom raised. 'It was a friendly voice even in anger. It did not matter what words he used to a defaulter, or in giving orders. The voice had a charm which endeared him to everyone, even if they did not realise it.'[3]

He served in the Naval Brigade during the Boer War and during the First World War in the Dardanelles commanding the destroyer *Scorpion* and took a minor part in the Zebrugge Raid in 1918. He became captain of the then new 34,000-ton battleship *Rodney* in 1929–1930. He was not a big-ship man at that time, having commanded nothing larger than a light cruiser.

Lieutenant Commander Geoffrey Oliver was the gunnery officer, and he found the ship to be a

> ... happy and successful one also. Bob Burnett the commander [Executive Officer] had an excellent way with the men, and it was a sad day when he and ABC [Cunningham] left at the same time ... [maybe] things would have gone differently in 1931 at Invergordon had they been there.[4]

However whether Cunningham was so understood, or even liked, at that time by the ordinary sailors and marines is a matter of conjecture for his 'tough managerial style was not always understood by members of the Lower Deck who found themselves joining up more out of economic necessity rather than a love of navy life.'[5]

In 1937 Cunningham commanded the Battlecruiser Squadron flying his flag in HMS *Hood*, having been promoted to Vice Admiral in 1936, in June 1939 becoming C-in-C Mediterranean Fleet.

There are mixed views on his temperament. General Sir Richard O'Conner thought him at his best, 'commanding the fleet in the Mediterranean' and he was 'the greatest sailor since Nelson.' Air Marshal

A. W. Tedder first met him in January 1941 and thought him quite athletic for his age with a lot of 'kick in the old boy yet.' However a year later he referred to him as 'the old man of the sea' and being 'rather a trial'.[6]

Ashore in Alexandria, Cunningham played tennis and golf when possible to keep fit. Many found him quite grumpy in harbour; Philip Vian, then a captain thought that 'the C-in-C ought to be put in a refrigerator as soon as we get back to harbour and not allowed out until we go to sea again.' Cunningham was a stickler for correct uniforms and a smart turn out. Wilfred Woods, then commanding a submarine, was picked up as his boat moved about the harbour of Alexandria because his crew looked like 'a lot of bloody pirates', although they were wearing the correct working rig for submarines.[7]

By noon on the 27th Cunningham knew, both from information gathered through visual sighting by the Sunderland flying boat of No 230 Squadron and codes via Ultra, that the Italian fleet was at sea. He resolved to take the fleet to sea under cover of darkness.

> I myself was inclined to think that the Italians would not dare to try anything. Later on we noticed some unusual Italian wireless activity, which finally decided us to go to sea after dark and place the battle fleet between the enemy and where we supposed our convoys must be. At the same time I bet Commander Power [Later Captain Manley L. Power] the staff officer, operations, the sum of ten shillings that we would see nothing of the enemy.[8]

Alexandria at that time was a hotbed of spies and informers. John Eppler had instigated a direct line from Egyptian nationalist groups like the Muslim Brotherhood, Ahmed Hussein's Young Egypt and members of Aziz El Masri's 'Ring of Iron' group in the Egyptian Army who aimed to rid Egypt of foreign rule, to the German Secret Service, which provided a steady stream of information; an unusual alliance indeed, but just one of several groups.[9]

Eppler was born in Germany shortly before the First World War. He was still a boy when his mother moved to Alexandria, and later married an Egyptian, Salah Gafaar. Gafaar adopted Eppler, made the boy a Muslim, and gave him the name Hussein Gafaar; he was sent to school in Europe, and approached by the Abwehr in 1937 and trained in Germany.[10]

British counter intelligence in Alexandria suspected the Japanese consul was responsible for reporting fleet movements to his interested allies. So Cunningham and his men

> ... decided to bluff this gentleman, so [I] went ashore to play golf carrying an obvious suit-case as though I intended to spend the night ashore. The Japanese Consul spent most of his afternoons on the golf links. He was unmistakable, indeed a remarkable sight, short, squat, with a southern aspect of such vast and elephantine proportions.[11]

Awnings were put out on the battleships, invitations to dinner on board made to aid the deception of the fleet staying in harbour. During the day several enemy reconnaissance aircraft were seen flying over Alexandria.

Cunningham was back on board by 19:00; there is a story of an Australian destroyer's motor boat giving a mysterious civilian-suited man a lift out to *Warspite*. The coxswain of the motor boat apparently agreed to the lift, but told the man whom he believed to be *Warspite's* canteen manager, that he would have to jump for the ladder as they passed *Warspite's* gangway; clutch trouble preventing him going astern. The passenger nimbly jumped as the boat passed the flagship's middle gangway. On reaching his own ship a signal arrived thanking him for the lift from the C-in-C. One wonders was this the evening of the 27th?[12]

About midday, the Vice-Admiral Light Forces (VALF), Vice-Admiral Pridham-Wippell, flying his flag in the cruiser *Orion* had left Piraeus after refuelling, with his cruisers and two destroyers *Hereward* and *Vendetta*. The other two destroyers *Ilex* and *Hasty* were at Suda Bay; they were ordered to leave there in time to rendezvous with the rest of the force on 28 March off the island of Gavdos. The day before, the cruiser *Gloucester* had run a bearing in a shaft which was replaced at Piraeus, but the divers found excessive slackness around an 'A' bracket which effectively reduced the ship's speed to 24 knots.

Pridham-Wippell was ordered to be 30 miles south of Gavdos Island by 06:30 with his four cruisers and four destroyers. Three additional destroyers at Piraeus were to remain there on standby. Greek naval forces were also on a high state of alert. The RAF promised maximum air reconnaissance over the southern Ionian and Aegean seas, and the sea south of Crete. Thirty bombers of 84, 113, and 211 Squadrons were on standby in Greece.

At Alexandria the battle fleet consisted of the battleships *Warspite* (flagship), *Barham* and *Valiant*, the latter fitted with radar, the new aircraft carrier *Formidable* also with radar and nine destroyers; 37 aircraft of the Fleet Air Arm were available.

Thirteen Fulmar fighters of 803 and 806 Squadrons and ten Albacores and four Swordfish of 826 and 829 Squadrons were embarked in *Formidable*; this was to be the carrier's first operation with the fleet. There were also five catapult aircraft with ships of the fleet. Five Swordfish of 815 Squadron, which had been with *Illustrious*, were now at Maleme in Crete.[13]

S. W. C. Pack was meteorological officer on board *Formidable* on Thursday 27 March.

> At 15:30 *Formidable* sailed, and about an hour later we turned into the wind to fly on the squadrons from Dekheila air-field. This was always an inspiring sight. It was a lovely spring afternoon, typical of the eastern Mediterranean at this time of the year. The sky was almost clear blue, except for a little tell-tale cirrus here and there, the wind was light. We were faced with few meteorological worries and no immediate flying difficulties.[14]

The fleet left Alexandria harbour at nightfall. *Warspite*, a ship with an already eventful history, chose that night to have another mishap. She sailed too close to a mud bank and stirred up the mud, contaminating her condensers. This reduced her speed and that of the battle fleet to 20 knots, which was later to cause some difficulty.

The fleet steered a north-westerly course at 20 knots and passed an uneventful night.

Notes
1 BBC World War II archives. Surgeon-Commander E.R. Sorley
2 Playfair, Major-General I.S.O. *The Mediterranean & Middle East Volume II* p.53
3 Pack, S.W.C. *Cunningham: The Commander* p.23
4 Ibid p.52
5 Ballantyne, Iain, *Rodney* p.61
6 Tedder, A.W. *Tedder with Prejudice* p.216
7 Pack, p.127–129
8 Cunningham, A.B. *A Sailor's Odyssey* p.326

9 Eppler, John, *Operation Condor: Rommel's Spy* p.40
10 Cooper, Artemis, *Cairo in the War 1939–1945* p.202–204
11 Cunningham, p.326
12 Pack, p.8
13 Playfair, p.62
14 Pack, S.W.C. *The Battle of Matapan* p.20

12

Daybreak, 28 March

On the afternoon of 27 March Admiral Iachino remained in something of a quandary because no further signals were intercepted from the Sunderland flying boat of 230 Squadron. Signals did come in from the British Naval Headquarters at Alexandria asking the Sunderland for further information but nothing further was heard from the crew, and he hoped that the crew had radio problems. However, at about 18:00 another signal from the Sunderland was intercepted, merely stating they had arrived at Corinth, had nothing further to report because of bad visibility, and they had maintained radio silence.

About the same time *Vittorio Veneto* received a signal from Supermarina reporting to the fleet commander they had intercepted the earlier message from the Sunderland. It was just as well Iachino had the foresight to have his own cipher staff on the flagship, and did not have to wait six hours for Supermarina to forward messages. It also contained the wrong information referring to the number of destroyers.

What caused Iachino even more concern was further information from the Naval High Command stating that because of weather conditions over Alexandria the afternoon air reconnaissance would not take place. Yet on board his radio intercepted a message from Aegean Air Command stating reconnaissance had been carried out over Alexandria at 14:00 and 14:45 confirming all the major units of the British Mediterranean Fleet were in harbour. It gave him no confidence in naval-air cooperation.[1]

By early evening Iachino was convinced that the British would withdraw all their convoys. They had intercepted several more British signals of the 'Immediate' category, which his cipher men had been unable to break. But it was plain to him and his staff that the British had issued a general alarm, but, perhaps, did not believe the threat required serious counter measures. The Admiral hoped Supermarina would be able to decode these signals, and would recall the fleet if they thought it in danger. However, this was extremely unlikely as Commander Bragadin explains.

> Supermarina was later criticised because with the element of surprise gone it did not call off the operation. But it must be remembered that this occasion was not born of a real tactical opportunity. Rather it was the result of a plan conceived under a press of considerations that were predominately political.[2]

The Fleet Commander only had a nominal command of his ships which were still controlled even at sea by Supermarina until contact was made with the enemy. He also had no control over the aircraft that were supposed to be supporting the fleet. In contrast Cunningham had complete command of his fleet and many air elements from the RAF as well.

The two Italian groups sailed on the evening of 27 March, the 1st and 8th Divisions proceeding toward the Aegean while *Vittorio Veneto* and the 3rd Division headed toward the south coast of Crete. However, at 22:00 Supermarina ordered the 1st and 8th Divisions to reverse course and join the flagship group the following morning. They had reached the same conclusion as Iachino: there was little chance of intercepting any convoys, and in view of this it was better to concentrate their forces.

Back on board the carrier *Formidable* some members of the crew were up before dawn to launch a weather balloon at 04:15 noting 'the sky was overcast but there was no rain.' The carrier needed an early weather report for flying operations and a weather map for the coming day. Much of the ship was still sleeping. 'Apart from the look-outs there were few on deck on this particular Friday morning, for it was still two hours to dawn.'[3] At 05:30 the air crews made their way to the carrier's island to enter the briefing room; it was still dark, with a hint of the coming light.

By 05:55 the fleet was 150 miles south of the eastern end of Crete. Light was growing from the east. *Formidable* turned into the wind to launch her dawn search aircraft. Roaring along the flight deck passing the bridge the pilots gave the thumbs up as their heavily fuelled aircraft lumbered into the air. Day was breaking, the clouds lifting and visibility was about fifteen miles.

At 06:00, Admiral Iachino gave orders for his catapult RO43 plane to be launched and to carry out reconnaissance. The rectangular area to be covered was 20 miles wide from the island of Gavdos and 100 miles toward Alexandria. The RO43 was not an ideal aircraft for the job, being slow and with a low endurance of five hours, and it could not be recovered from the sea by the mother ship, so had to fly on to land bases. In this case after the mission the aircraft would fly on to Leros.[4]

At this time *Vittorio Veneto* was sailing toward the target area. The 3rd Cruiser Division was off her port bow ten miles distant, the 1st and 8th Divisions were about fifteen miles behind to the port.

By 06:30 all the cruiser squadrons were visible from the flagship. Iachino ordered Admiral Cattaneo's 1st Cruiser Division to take up station ten miles to the north of *Vittorio Veneto* and all ships to increase speed to 25 knots.

Admiral Iachino patiently pacing the bridge of his flagship decided if nothing was seen by 07:00 the fleet would return to base. However at 06:35, *Vittorio Veneto*'s RO43 reported a force of four cruisers and four destroyers sailing at 18 knots southeast about 50 miles from the fleet. He ordered the 3rd Division – his most advanced force – to make contact while he would support them with the flagship.

At 07:22 aircraft from *Formidable* also reported four cruisers and four destroyers; they had sighted the 1st and 8th Divisions, some 35 miles northeast of VALF. Another *Formidable* aircraft shortly after this reported three cruisers and six destroyers 25 miles southeast from the first sighting; this was the 3rd Division. Both Cunningham and Pridham-Wippell at first thought these reports related to the latter's ships and were therefore friendly forces.

Admiral Iachino had cancelled orders to return to base. He even briefly had renewed hopes of finding a convoy. *Vittorio Veneto* increased speed to 28 knots to support the 3rd Cruiser Division that was heading south at 31 knots, while Admiral Cattaneo's force also increased speed.

At 07:58 the 3rd Division sighted VALF's group. About 08:30 Pridham-Wippell reported three enemy cruisers and destroyers to the north of his position. Cunningham had lost his bet. 'This made it clear that the enemy fleet was at sea, so I cheerfully paid up my ten shillings.'[5]

The British battle fleet was about 90 miles southeast of VALF's force steaming toward them at 20 knots. 'Admiral Sansonetti continued to follow the British ships at high speed, and at 08:12, from a range of about 25,000 metres, he opened fire. Thus began the encounter of Gavdos.'[6]

Notes

1 Bragadin, M.A. *The Italian Navy in World War II* p.85
2 Ibid p.86
3 Pack, S.W.C. *The Battle of Matapan* p.38
4 Bragadin, p.86
5 Cunningham, A.B. *A Sailor's Odyssey* p.327
6 Bragadin, M.A. p.86–87

Left: HMS *Valiant* leads the line as the Italian fleet steams into Malta, under the terms of the armistice, seen from the aft deck of HMS *Warspite.* (USN Historical Centre No SC188574)

Below: Two views of Fort Rinella on Malta, and the 100-ton Armstrong gun. (Author)

Two views of the battleship *Roma*, last of the *Littorio* class battleships completed in 1942. (Italian Navy Historical Archives)

HMS *Ark Royal* in 1939 with Swordfish aircraft on the flight deck. She was the first of Britain's purpose-built aircraft carriers. (Royal Navy Museum)

The floating dock of Malta, taken from the Baccara Gardens. This dock was the replacement for that lost during the Second World War. (A.F.T. Simmons collection)

HMS *Warspite* entering Malta. (A.F.T. Simmons collection)

The battleship *Caio Duilio*. She entered service in 1915, seen here still with her central Q turret which she lost during modernisation in the mid 1930s. (Italian Navy Historical Archives)

Opposite: A reconnaissance photograph of the outer harbour at Taranto taken by the RAF the day before the operation. Five battleships can be clearly seen. (Fleet Air Arm Museum)

HMS *Illustrious* underway. (Fleet Air Arm Museum)

TARANTO 10·11·40
(L) = LITTORIO CLASS BATTLES
(C) = CAVOUR

Conte di Cavour, the third Italian battleship to be hit, sitting on the bottom of Taranto outer harbour the day after the attack. (Italian Navy Historical Archives)

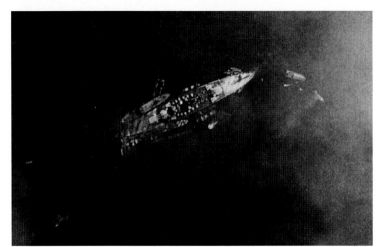

Littorio on the bottom, four days after the attack on Taranto. (Fleet Air Arm Museum)

The Italian heavy cruisers *Pola*, *Fiume*, and *Zara* moored by the stern at Taranto. They were all later sunk at Matapan. (Italian Navy Historical Archives)

Littorio, the salvage operation well underway at Taranto. (Italian Navy Historical Archives)

HMS *Illustrious* under heavy attack. (Fleet Air Arm Museum I/P43)

Gun director crew take a rest on HMS *Gloucester* during the battle for Crete. (Royal Navy Museum)

The *Vittorio Veneto* at sea.
(Italian Navy Historical
Archives)

Italian heavy cruiser *Zara*
sunk at Matapan. (Royal Navy
Museum)

Heavy cruiser HMS *Kent* at Suda Bay on Crete after an attack by Regia Marina special forces. (Italian Navy Historical Archives)

Grand Harbour, Malta. Britain made every effort to hold the island, which was the key to the Mediterranean. (Author)

The Italian
heavy cruisers
Zara, Pola, Fiume
and *Garibaldi*
steaming at
speed on the
morning of 28
March. (Royal
Navy Museum)

Admiral Angelo
Iachino (centre)
on board his
flagship *Vittorio
Veneto*. RO43
floatplane on its
launch system in
the background.
(Italian Navy
Historical
Archives)

Italian destroyers
escorting *Vittorio
Veneto* during
the Matapan
operation.
(Italian Navy
Historical
Archives)

The aircraft carrier HMS *Formidable*, as seen from *Warspite*. (Royal Navy Museum)

HMS *Formidable* at flying stations. (Royal Navy Museum)

Swordfish taking off in a torpedo strike role. (Royal Navy Museum)

HMS *Warspite* opens fire on Italian ships as they are illuminated. (Dennis C. Andrews)

British battleships open fire, taken from *Valiant* with *Barham* and *Warspite* ahead. (Royal Navy Museum)

Immaculate as usual. Admiral Sir Andrew Browne Cunningham, on *Warspite* with HMS *Eagle* in the background. (Fleet Air Arm Museum Pers/315)

Left: Admiral Angelo Iachino on board his flagship *Vittorio Veneto*. (Royal Navy Museum)

Right: The pom-pom crew relax after air attack on board the cruiser HMS *Gloucester*. (Royal Navy Museum)

British cruisers at sea from HMS *Gloucester* during the Matapan battle. (Royal Navy Museum)

Admiral Angelo Iachino takes the salute. (Italian Navy Historical Archives)

The diving and power controls of an Italian two-man torpedo, a 'pig'. (Author)

Italian two-man *Maiale* or pig, so-called because it was so difficult to steer, seen here inside its carrying pod, which was strapped to a conventional submarine for transportation. (Author)

Two-man submarine diver's rig. (Author)

HMS *Valiant* underway; the battleship was badly damaged during the Italian two-man submarine attack at Alexandria. (Royal Navy Museum)

13

Morning, 28 March

At 07:34 *Vittorio Veneto* signalled Admiral Sansonetti aboard *Trieste*. 'After sighting enemy retire towards me.' The destroyers escorting the battle-ship were ordered to move from their starboard station to port to clear *Vittorio Veneto's* field of fire. At 07:43 action stations were sounded.

Sighting the British force, Sansonetti found they turned away at high speed, so he gave chase opening fire at a range of thirteen miles.

Vice-Admiral Pridham-Wippell soon realised he was outgunned, and that the Italian cruisers were as fast, if not faster than his own ships. He was hoping to lure the enemy toward his own supporting battle fleet. Admiral Sansonetti's ships were steaming near top speed at 31 knots, whereas the VALF's squadron speed was 23 knots; the range was closing.

The Italians concentrated their fire on the last ship of the British line, *Gloucester*, which began to zigzag. After fifteen minutes she opened fire with her 6-inch guns; all salvoes up to this point had fallen short. *Gloucester* also flew off her aircraft for observation, but the pilot was using the wrong radio frequency and his signals were not received by the *Orion*, Pridham-Wippell's flagship.[1]

The Italians continued to fire while moving out of range of *Gloucester's* guns. The cruiser had overcome her engine troubles and the British cruis-ers had worked up to 28 knots, but about this time the destroyer *Vendetta* developed engine trouble and began lagging behind. Pridham-Wippell ordered her to steer to the south away from the action and then return to Alexandria. The destroyers, the all-duty workhorses of the fleet, were in short supply and essential to everything. Lack of destroyers hampered Cunningham's operations, as noted by John Lee-Barber of the *Griffin*.

As usual ABC had to scrape the bucket for destroyers to go to sea and *Griffin*, having been holed in all the forward oil fuel tanks by a bomb in Malta some days previously, went on the operation [Matapan] with oil fuel only in the after tanks, the forward ones being open to the sea.[2]

J.E. MacDonnell of HMAS *Stuart*:

The day before the victory at Matapan HMAS *Stuart* was lying up in Alexandria waiting to be docked. A near miss off Benghazi had blown half her rudder off. Then a string of flags was hauled up *Warspite's* foremast. It was a general signal from Admiral Cunningham, and it read; 'Raise steam for full speed with all dispatch.'[3]

The Italians suffered as much as the British in this regard. Their destroyers were probably, on the whole, not so hardworking but tended often to be older to start with.

Admiral Sansonetti's ships continued to steam parallel to the British, keeping up their fire until 08:55, when they turned away to port breaking off the action. Admiral Iachino had ordered the 3rd Division to reverse course and the whole fleet would return to base. 'It seemed, all in all, a useless risk to continue this vain firefight, particularly since the Italian ships had already gone far beyond Gavdos, and were almost half way to Tobruk.'[4]

Iachino was puzzled by the British tactics, and the fact that the action was being drawn farther south, when in his experience his enemy did not usually avoid battle in an action where the odds were not that great, for it seemed from the radio traffic that they were unaware of *Vittorio Veneto*. He believed they were trying to draw them into an area for attack by British aircraft, while no friendly air cover had turned up.

The destroyer *Pessagno* was experiencing boiler trouble and had to reduce speed to 25 knots. About this time Admiral Iachino ordered the fleet to concentrate on the flagship and set course on 300° to the west.

About 08:54 the VALF received news from *Formidable* aircraft that 50 minutes earlier they had sighted a force of three battleships steering southwest at 20 knots. Pridham-Wippell found this hard to believe. He had been very near the position reported and must have seen these ships. Rear Admiral Boyd (Air) on *Formidable* agreed with him that the aircraft had mistakenly identified cruisers as battleships, however warning he could not completely reject the possibility of Italian heavy units being at sea nearby. When Admiral Sansonetti broke off the action steering northwest with his 3rd Division, the VALF turned about, shadowing the Italian ships.

At 10:35 Admiral Iachino changed his mind again. As no British ships or aircraft seemed aware of *Vittorio Veneto* he reversed the battleship's course. He hoped to catch the British cruisers between the flagship and the 3rd Division. At 10:50 *Vittorio Veneto* sighted the VALF ships; Iachino ordered the 3rd Division to reverse course while at 10:56, at 25,000 metres, the battleship's 15-inch guns opened fire.

About 70 miles southeast of VALF, the British battle fleet received news at about 08:27 from Admiral Pridham-Wippell that he had sighted the enemy. Admiral Cunningham altered course towards him and increased speed to 22 knots, dictated by *Warspite's* condenser troubles. *Warspite* and *Valiant* began to pull ahead of *Barham* and *Formidable*, which was preparing to fly off strike aircraft. The situation was unclear to Cunningham, but fearing the VALF might be in danger, at 09:39 he ordered an air torpedo striking force. Six Albacores of 826 and 829 Squadrons with an escort of two Fulmar fighters were flown off from *Formidable*.[5] Another strike force was readied at Maleme, but delays in signals and waiting for aircraft to return from patrols meant the three Swordfish of this force did not take off until 10:50.

At last, at 10:58 the *Orion* spotted one *Vittorio Veneto* class battleship about fifteen miles to the north. Admiral Pridham-Wippell, once he had identified the ship, altered course south making smoke and increased speed to maximum in an attempt to disengage. The chase was on again. However, the British cruisers were under bombardment for 30 minutes, as the official history says '15-inch salvoes, which though desultory was at times uncomfortably accurate.'[6] *Orion* did receive considerable damage from a near miss.

Aboard the *Warspite* Cunningham felt the situation was becoming alarming.

We knew that the '*Littorio*' [also known as *Vittorio Veneto*] class of battleship was capable of 31 knots, and the night before, because of engine trouble, the *Gloucester* had reported herself capable of no more than 24. There was another strong enemy cruiser squadron to the northward of Pridham-Wippell. However, the sight of an enemy battleship had somehow increased the *Gloucester's* speed to 30 knots.[7]

Cunningham was frustrated by *Warspite's* lack of speed; he ordered *Valiant* to go on at her 'utmost speed', while he sent Fleet Engineer Officer Captain B.J.H.Wilkinson below in the flagship to see what he could do.'In a short time I was gratified to see the *Valiant*, which had been coming up at full speed from astern, was no longer gaining. We pressed on together.'[8] The C-in-C had hoped to hold the air strike until he was closer, but felt his hand was forced by the danger to VALF, and ordered the strike to go in as soon as possible.

Admiral Iachino had closed the range beyond his best 25,000 metres for *Vittorio Veneto's* guns because of bad visibility.The three main turrets in the battleship were firing in rapid succession at different elevations – 'ladder fire' – trying to find the range.VALF responded by turning 90° to port and began making smoke and to zigzag. *Gloucester* at the end of the line, being less covered by the smokescreen became the main target.

Shortly before 11:00 lookouts on *Vittorio Veneto* reported six aircraft approaching from astern. At first they were thought to be Italian from Rhodes, but as they came closer they were identified as British. They flew parallel to the Italian ships, then moved away to organise into an attack formation.

At 11:15 the Albacores of *Formidable's* first strike came in low over the sea.The main armament of *Vittorio Veneto* ceased firing, while the ship prepared to meet the air attack, the anti-aircraft batteries already firing. The torpedo bombers came in at an angle about 30 feet above the sea trying to aim at the battleship's bows. Lieutenant F.H.E. Hopkins was observer aboard Albacore 4A flown by Lieutenant Commander Gerald Saunt.

> Eventually we got into an attacking position and the first flight of three aircraft dived to the starboard bow of the target and dropped torpedoes. As the *Vittorio* turned to comb the tracks she was caught beam on by the second flight of three aircraft. At least one torpedo hit and *Vittorio Veneto* circled through 360° and apparently stopped.[9]

Iachino at his 'action station' in the armoured control turret ordered the rudders put hard to starboard. He could see little from his position so returned to the bridge; by the time he reached there he could see the tracks of the torpedoes had passed astern of the ship.The enemy aircraft then withdrew. By now he was convinced he would have no air support.

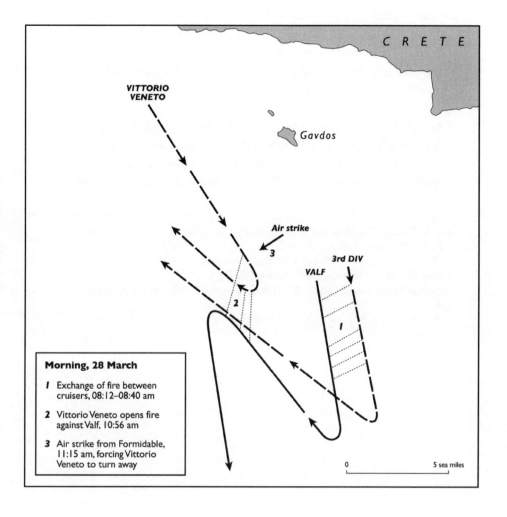

C R E T E

VITTORIO
VENETO

Gavdos

Air strike

3

3rd DIV

VALF

2

1

Morning, 28 March

1 Exchange of fire between
   cruisers, 08:12–08:40 am

2 Vittorio Veneto opens fire
   against Valf, 10:56 am

3 Air strike from Formidable,
   11:15 am, forcing Vittorio
   Veneto to turn away

0   5 sea miles

At 11:30 *Vittorio Veneto,* undamaged, changed course to 300° and the fleet headed for home.

The Albacores from *Formidable* had been attacked by two Junkers JU 88 fighter bombers, but the Fulmars shot one down and drove the other off. The first strike reported once back on *Formidable* that they were convinced they had hit *Vittorio Veneto*, at least once, maybe more.

VALF was unaware that the Italians had come under air attack, but realised that they had broken off the action. By 11:38 *Gloucester* informed him the enemy had moved away to the north. Pridham-Wippell therefore set course to join the battle fleet, with which he made visual contact about 12:30.[10]

At 12:07 the three swordfish from Crete attacked the 3rd Division cruisers concentrating on *Bolzano*, the rear ship of the group. Coming out of the sun for a bow shot, again all three Mark 12 torpedoes missed. Despite heavy anti-aircraft fire from the ships no aircraft were lost.

Notes

1 Seth, Ronald, *Two Fleets Surprised: The Battle of Matapan* p.56
2 Pack, S.W.C. *The Battle of Matapan* p.128
3 MacClonnell, J.E. *As you Were*, www.diggerhistory.au
4 Bragadin, M.A. *The Italian Navy in World War II* p.88
5 Playfair, Major-General I.S.O. *The Mediterranean and Middle East Volume II* p.64
6 Ibid p.64
7 Cunningham, A.B. *A Sailor's Odyssey* p.327
8 Ibid p.328
9 Pack, p.66
10 Playfair, p.64

14

Afternoon, 28 March

After a Herculean effort by the crew of *Formidable*, at 11:55 the Rear Admiral Air was able to report to the C-in-C that the second strike force was ready. It was made up of aircraft that had been on reconnaissance duties earlier in the morning; the last Swordfish of that mission had landed back on the carrier at 11:30, requiring refuelling and arming with a torpedo.

Cunningham ordered Boyd to hold the second strike. This order presented Boyd with a problem as the first strike force was on its way back to the carrier, while the flight deck was ranged with the second strike aircraft. It would mean delays if this force was put below. Therefore he asked Cunningham for permission to fly off the second strike and recover the first. The C-in-C agreed, so around 12:00 *Formidable* hauled out of line, flying off the second strike of three Albacores and two Swordfish of 829 Squadron, with two Fulmar escort fighters. They had orders to stay over the fleet to see if the ships became engaged; if this did not happen by 13:30, they were to locate and attack the enemy themselves.

Formidable had completed this operation, which meant detaching herself from the fleet, by 12:44, but it took her until 14:00 to catch up. She was attacked by two S79s – Italian torpedo bombers – during this time. They came in low under the fighter patrol but they failed to hit the carrier.

At 12:25 *Warspite* and *Valiant* flew off their Swordfish float aircraft for reconnaissance during the expected action, two from each ship. *Warspite*'s A aircraft was to act as observer while B would spot for the flagship's guns. *Valiant*'s aircraft were to spot for *Valiant* and *Barham*. *Warspite*'s

B aircraft and both of *Valiant*'s were to fly on to Suda Bay once they reached their fuel-endurance limit.

When VALF made contact with the battle fleet at 12:30 *Vittorio Veneto* was farther away than Cunningham had thought, some 65 miles to the west. The strong north-easterly wind had dropped, easing flying operations.[1]

The Swordfish float plane K 8863 'Lorna' had left *Warspite* at 12:15, as the observer aircraft. She was flown by PO Ben Rice, with Maurice Pacey as her TAG and Lieutenant-Commander A.S. Bolt as the observer. Bolt noted:

> The main forces were meeting at high speed. The battle fleet steering to support the cruiser squadron at 23 knots was expected to make contact with the advanced units of the Italian fleet within at most two hours when *Warspite* launched my aircraft for action observation. My duties were to obtain a visual link between the fleets as soon as possible and then report generally on the tactical situation as seen from the air.[2]

Shortly after this Cunningham was made aware by VALF that the Italians were much farther away than he had expected.

After the first torpedo bomber attack on the Italian fleet, Admiral Iachino set course for Taranto. He was disappointed with the results of the surface action, where he had held the advantage for a while. *Vittorio Veneto* had fired 29 salvoes, 94 shells from her 15-inch guns, without registering a major hit. Eleven shells had misfired and the salvoes' spread was too great; they often straddled a target but were unable to tighten the spread. The 3rd Cruiser Division had done no better, having fired hundreds of 8-inch shells with no hits. This was chiefly, as Iachino knew, the result of a lack of training and technical skill and could not be practically addressed with the disadvantages under which the fleet operated. Admiral Iachino was still ignorant at this time that the British battle fleet was at sea and so close. He felt he was unlikely to encounter any more British surface units, but expected more air attacks.[3]

About 14:00 Admiral Cunningham issued a special signal to the fleet of his appreciation of the situation. The Italian fleet appeared divided into two groups, northern and southern. The southern consisted of one battleship, three cruisers and seven destroyers, which had last been seen around 11:15 by VALF, and had been attacked by the *Formidable* first strike. The northern group appeared to consist of two battleships (an erroneous identification as all were cruisers) three cruisers and destroyers. This had been attacked by the Maleme strike force from Crete, west of Gavdos Island steering west.

> We settled down to a chase, and it was clear enough that it would be a long one and without reward unless the *Vittorio Veneto* was damaged and slowed by our aircraft attacks. The pursuit was made even longer as speed had to be reduced to 22 knots to allow the *Formidable* to rejoin and the *Barham* to keep up. But we had one providential piece of good fortune. The easterly wind dropped and it became flat calm with occasional light airs from the westward, which meant that the *Formidable* could carry out all her flying operations from her station in the line.[4]

A shortage of reconnaissance aircraft meant they had lost contact with the Italian fleet altogether. Three Albacores of 826 Squadron, part of *Formidable's* first strike, were refuelled and sent out to search at 14:00. About 15:00, Lieutenants Ellis and Haworth of aircraft 4F sighted *Vittorio Veneto*, and at about 15:15 they were able to give the battleship's position and speed.

Ten minutes later the second *Formidable* strike force sighted *Vittorio Veneto* with two destroyers on each side. The squadron commander, Lieutenant-Commander J. Dalyell-Stead 5G, prepared to attack.

Throughout the day, Admiral Iachino received more conflicting signals. About noon Supermarina informed him the British Fleet was still in Alexandria, and the only forces in his area were the four cruisers, which he had recently engaged. This was a relayed signal from Italian Air Command on Rhodes which was hours out of date, having been transmitted from Rhodes to Italian Air Force Command in Rome, then to Supermarina and finally to Iachino. Two more signals came in about the same time, one from X Cat German Air Command in Sicily and one from Supermarina, informing him that *Formidable* was at sea and it was her aircraft that had attacked him, by then something he was well aware of. He found it odd that *Formidable* was at sea on her own, but reasoned that the German spotter plane must surely have seen the battleships if they were at sea. Of course *Formidable* at that time was detached for flying operations, and the aircraft did not see the rest of the fleet.

The Italian fleet continued to withdraw west. About 14:30, a delayed message from Rhodes arrived, timed at 12:25. 'Aircraft 1 Aegean Strategic Reconnaissance sighted one battleship; one carrier, six cruisers, and five destroyers sector 5647.'⁵ This put the enemy 80 miles to the east, and Iachino began to wonder if the Rhodes aircraft was reporting his own ships. All he could do was continue on his present course and speed and see what Supermarina had to say. About 15:00 a D/F intercept (direction finding on radio transmissions) came in, putting the enemy 110 miles 60° from Tobruk, 170 miles away, transmitting to Crete and Alexandria. Were these the same ships the Rhodes aircraft had seen? If so it could not be his ships mistakenly identified as British. Also these ships transmitting to Crete and Alexandria made them fairly important.

Iachino reached the conclusion that there must be two British groups at sea: the cruisers and a battleship carrier group. Were they apart or together and where, 80 or 170 miles away? He felt a D/F bearing was likely to be more reliable than the eyes of the aircraft crew, so he took the 170-mile distance as correct.

These conflicting messages were confusing Iachino and his staff, due mainly to delays in transmission. However, mistrust of the Regia Aeronautica and Luftwaffe may have clouded his judgement, as the aircraft report he rejected in favour of the D/F report was sent by an aircraft within sight of land, so the observers would have been well aware of their position. In contrast the D/F bearing was inaccurate due to instrument malfunction or lack of operator skill.

For unexplained reasons Supermarina did not decode Cunningham's signals to Crete ordering the Fleet Air Arm there to attack the Italian fleet at dusk. However Iachino had rightly identified his greatest danger would come from the air. The 3rd Cruiser Division had been attacked, and by 14:20 the *Vittorio Veneto* group had been hit twice, once by *Formidable*'s first strike and then by three RAF Blenheims of 84 Squadron based in Greece. The latter group had dropped bombs but no hits were made, but another six Blenheims from 113 Squadron attacked at 14:50. These attacks by the RAF were making history, for in effect Admiral Cunningham, through arrangements with the bases at Menidi and Paranythia, had these aircraft under command standing by.

Admiral Iachino was justifiably upset by the total lack of air cover his ships received. 'I felt pretty well deceived by the lack of cooperation. We continued to remain for the rest of the day without any fighter cover.' X

Cat on Sicily replied to repeated requests from Iachino and Supermarina for air cover, saying 'it could not go out on such missions because there was a danger that its planes might accidentally attack the Italian ships, since the position of the British ships was not known.'[6]

The second Blenheim attack came in shortly before *Formidable's* second strike led by Lieutenant-Commander Dalyell-Stead. On sighting the *Vittorio Veneto* he led the three Albacores and two Swordfish into the sun to get down to 5,000 feet before he was seen. One Italian destroyer soon spotted them and opened fire. The Fulmars strafed the ship trying to keep their fire down. The three Albacores flew on through the destroyer screen to some 3,000 yards ahead of the *Vittorio Veneto* then breaking formation, two turning to port and one to starboard; turning about they came at the ship from three different angles.

Iachino believed the high-level bombers had distracted his gunners until the torpedo bombers were close, and admired the coordination. The Fulmars also strafed the battleship's upper works and bridges, momentarily scattering the anti-aircraft gunners. Thus the three Albacores continued their approach with not so much attention from anti-aircraft fire.

They came in fast above the waves trying to keep level to release their torpedoes and let them run true. Men on the *Vittorio Veneto* reported that the aircraft came in about 1,000 yards before dropping their torpedoes; as the ship was healing over to starboard they could see the tracks in the water. 5G Dalyell-Stead's aircraft was hit by a barrage of fire as he crossed in front of the ship's course and the anti-aircraft gunners came to life. His aircraft was fatally hit a dozen yards ahead of the battleship's bows, crashing into the sea 1,000 yards out on the starboard side. All three of the crew – Lieutenant-Commander Dalyell-Stead, Lieutenant Cooke the observer and PO Blenkhorn the air gunner – were killed. With the turn of the ship the torpedo track was heading toward the stern, and within seconds of the death of the crew of 5G their torpedo hit home. 'The screws on the port side took the blow. For a time the ship was unable to move, and 4000 tons of water poured in through the breach.'[7]

Mike Haworth was watching in his reconnaissance role with 4F from *Formidable* and wrote of the attack.

The attack was delivered in two waves because the Albacores in the striking force climbed at a higher speed than the Swordfish. Diving out of the sun, the leading sub flight appeared to achieve a degree of surprise and the enemy made a turn of 180° to avoid them.

He saw 'smoke rings from the funnel, and a further, 180° turn to revert to the original retreating course.' However the speed of the *Vittorio Veneto*, he felt, was much reduced.[8]

The two Swordfish saw the *Vittorio Veneto*'s turn to starboard away from her destroyer screen, so they dived down from 8,000 feet to attack the starboard side. By the time they reached sea level the ship's speed had dropped by half. This presented the aircraft with an easier shot, but the anti-aircraft fire had grown in intensity, and no hits were scored.

At about the same time as the torpedo attacks were going on against *Vittorio Veneto*, Blenheims from RAF Squadrons 113 and 84 attacked the 3rd Cruiser Division; they claimed three hits on two ships but all were near misses. Further attacks came in against Admiral Cattaneo's 1st Cruiser Division, but again only near misses were achieved on the *Zara* and *Garibaldi* causing no damage. These tailed off about 17:00 by which time six Blenheims from 211 Squadron had also attacked the Italian fleet.

About this time Lieutenant-Commander Bolt on board *Warspite*'s Swordfish K 8863 observer float plane was still airborne. 'My routine reports of fuel state evoked no response from HMS *Warspite*, until I reported only fifteen minutes of fuel remaining.' The aircraft could not reach Suda Bay, by now over an hour's flying time away. The fleet was steaming flat out in pursuit of *Vittorio Veneto* which had been slowed by *Formidable*'s second strike, and did not want to slow to recover an aircraft, a fact Bolt was well aware of.

> My aircraft was ordered to alight ahead of *Warspite* in the grain of the fleet. With the crane swung out on the starboard side, the plan was to hook on as the ship steamed up to overtake the aircraft, taxiing on a parallel course.

Luckily for PO Rice, the pilot, the sea was flat calm, and they began to taxi ahead of the ship at ten knots with the 30,000-ton battleship *Warspite* coming up astern at 20 knots.

> We had never practised this method of recovery and were a good deal disturbed by the bow wave. However, I was able to con PO

Rice to a position under the grab hook and Lieutenant-Commander Copeman, with whom I had a good understanding in the recovery operation hoisted us quickly clear of the water as soon as I gave the hooked-on signal.

The aircraft was put straight back on the catapult and refuelled. Bolt found out later *Warspite* had still been steaming at 18 knots throughout the recovery process.

At 17:45 less than an hour after coming back on board, *Warspite's* Swordfish K 8863 took to the air again. According to PO Pacey the TAG, 'The last thing I did before take-off was to grab three flame floats as I realised that we were going to have to alight at night on the open sea with no organised flame-path.'[9]

At Maleme on Crete the men of 815 Squadron Fleet Air Arm were hard at work; as soon as their first strike returned at 13:30 they tried to get another ready, but were short of aircraft. Also communications were difficult, since the cruiser *York* had been badly damaged. Maleme airfield had a small transmitter-receiver but it had a limited range. To try and get more information a Fulmer was sent out to try and find *Vittorio Veneto* and check her position, course and speed before launching a second strike.

Lieutenant Michael Torrens-Spence:

> On 28 March, when we were refitting at Eieusis because of no moon, I was ordered to Crete with all available torpedo-armed aircraft, which amounted to just two. We landed at Maleme in Crete at about noon and given a position, course and speed of the Italian fleet … We took off at 17:00 for a dusk attack.[10]

He had brought with him the last remaining torpedo in Greece. Admiral Cunningham's surface fleet had had no visual contact of the enemy since *Vittorio Veneto* had broken off the action minutes before noon. Aircraft reports had come in thick and fast during the afternoon but were confused concerning the composition and disposition of the Italian fleet.

> It now became necessary to establish surface touch with the enemy, so at 4:44p.m. Vice Admiral Pridham-Wippell was ordered to press on at full speed and get into visual touch with the retreating enemy. The

destroyers *Nubian* and *Mowhawk* were also sent ahead to form a visual signal link between Pridham-Wippell's cruisers and the battle fleet.[11]

Cunningham wisely began organising his forces for the possibility of night action. A striking force of eight destroyers under Captain Philip Mack of the *Jervis* were to be on hand if the cruisers of VALF made contact with *Vittorio Veneto* to launch a night torpedo attack; if necessary, he was willing to commit his battleships to night action. If his ships failed to make contact he intended to work round to the north and northwest hoping to catch the *Vittorio Veneto* at dawn. He also ordered *Formidable* to launch another air strike at dusk. However by now *Formidable* was running short of aircraft, she recalled all her search aircraft except 4F Lieutenant Ellis who continued shadowing the Italian fleet.

Around 16:00 the *Vittorio Veneto* was underway but with greatly reduced speed; in fact at 15:30 she had stopped altogether. She was listing to port and was down by the stern. The explosion of the torpedo had broken the main shaft of the outer port engine; the inner port engine's lubricating system was contaminated by sea water causing the suspension bearings of the shaft to seize up. This meant that only the starboard engines were working, and the vessel had to be steered by keeping the rudders to starboard and this had to be done by hand. However, by 17:00 – much to the credit of her engineering staff – she was making 19 knots.

Admiral Iachino was 420 miles from Taranto, a fair distance to go in a crippled ship that was hard to manoeuvre. He expected more air attacks before nightfall and destroyer attacks by night. At 16:15 he received an air sighting report of British destroyers reaching west from the Cerigotta channel. He was sure that Admiral Cunningham had ordered these ships from Suda Bay to attack him.

He still had little idea the British battle fleet was so close and closing on him. To combat possible air and destroyer attacks he decided to form his fleet into a defensive box with *Vittorio Veneto* at the centre with cruisers and destroyers on both sides. They would then be able to put up a wall of anti-aircraft fire. If aircraft came he expected them at dusk, when he would also use smokescreens. After nightfall he would change course to try and shake off any pursing destroyers.

The Italian fleet formed into five lines, with *Vittorio Veneto* in the centre, two destroyers ahead and two astern. The 3rd Cruiser Division took up station on the port beam 1,000 yards away leading *Trento*, followed by *Trieste* and *Bolzano*, with three destroyers a further 1,000 yards out forming an outer screen. On the starboard beam formed Admiral Cattaneo's 1st Cruiser Division ships in which Iachino had served. He had been in *Zara* during the Abyssinian war and *Pola* had been his own flagship until December 1940. He knew the officers and men; the Captain, De Pisa, had been his own flag captain, a capable officer and friend. *Fiume* had been his flagship in 1938 at the naval review in Naples. The ill-fated squadron was special to him. Four destroyers formed the outer screen, while the light cruisers *Abruzzi* and *Garibaldi* were instructed to return to their base at Brindisi. By 18:00 all the ships were in position.[12]

Vittorio Veneto was still listing although the pumps kept the flooding down; her starboard engines were working normally. The possibility of sea water entering their lubricating system was a constant worry. However another problem came up; a signal intercepted by *Vittorio Veneto*'s cipher experts revealed an air attack was to be carried out against them at sunset by aircraft from Crete. Supermarina did not forward this signal to Iachino until 21:00, by which time the attack was over.

About 18:23 the first enemy aircraft was spotted astern keeping their distance, circling like vultures waiting for dusk. It soon became clear that there were nine aircraft.[13]

Notes
1 Playfair, Major-General I.S.O. *The Mediterranean and Middle East Volume II* p.64
2 Poolman, Kenneth, *Experiences of War: The British Sailor* p.125
3 Bragadin, M.A. *The Italian Navy in World War II* p.89
4 Cunningham, A.B. *A Sailor's Odyssey* p.329
5 Bragadin, p.101
6 Ibid p.90
7 Ibid p.90
8 Pack, S.W.C. *The Battle of Matapan* p.83
9 Poolman, p.125–126
10 Arthur, Max, *Lost Voices of the Royal Navy* p.270
11 Cunningham, p.329
12 Seth, Ronald, *Two Fleets Surprised: The Battle of Matapan* p.96
13 Bragadin, p.91

15

Attack at Dusk

I shall go at them at once, if I can, about one-third of the line from
their leading ship ... I think it will surprise and confound the enemy
... It will bring on a pell-mell battle, and that is what I want.
Vice-Admiral Lord Nelson off Cape Trafalgar, October 1805.[1]

At 18:20 *Warspite*'s Swordfish, with Bolt on board. sighted the *Vittorio
Veneto*. He estimated her speed at 12–15 knots. At this speed it would
take the British battle fleet at least four hours to get within gun range
so all now rested on the destroyer attack, and *Formidable*'s third strike,
to slow the enemy further. Bolt kept sending out a stream of messages,
which *Vittorio Veneto* was soon reading. They were surprised at the accu-
racy of his messages regarding speed and course.

The aircraft which had been spotted by Italian lookouts were
Formidable's third strike force, commanded by Lieutenant-Commander
W.H.G. Saunt in 4A composed of six Albacores of 826 Squadron and two
Swordfish of 829 Squadron. They were soon joined by two Swordfish
from Maleme, Crete, of 815 Squadron. According to Lieutenant Michael
Torrens-Spence:

My young observer, Sub-Lieutenant Peter Winter, did a good job and
found the enemy. Before attacking we had to circle for a long time
until the light conditions were right. While doing so a mixture of
eight Swordfish and Albacores ... arrived from *Formidable*, flying in
line at low level.[2]

The Fulmar fighter sent out to find *Vittorio Veneto* from Maleme returned about 16:00 with the location. Three Swordfish took off for the strike, but one developed engine trouble and had to turn back at about 17:15. The sea was calm, the evening fine as the aircraft circled waiting for the sun to sink in the west, the Italian ships below steaming steadily on.

About 18:15 Admiral Iachino ordered his fleet to change course 30° to port to try and shake off the aircraft. The two destroyers astern of the flagship began to make smoke. To avoid ramming the two destroyers ahead he ordered them to move 10°, one to port and one to starboard and they began making smoke, while the cruisers turned on their search-lights to blind the attacking pilots.[3]

Alpino, the last destroyer of the centre column, reported the aircraft were beginning their approach. By 19:30 it was almost dark although the ships were clearly silhouetted against the western sky. Iachino ordered the fleet to again change course 30° to starboard bringing the fleet back onto its original course. Soon the destroyers began firing, and then the cruisers joined in. Lieutenant Michael Torrens-Spence watched the *Formidable's* aircraft attack:

> The enemy was in very close formation with all ships making smoke which obliged Saunt's aircraft to drop their torpedoes in succession outside the smoke screen.
>
> At that time we still had no radio communication between aircraft, so that, even if Saunt could have thought out a better tactic, he had no means of ordering it.

The Maleme aircraft were free to attack as they saw fit. Torrens-Spence found a gap in the smokescreen into which he dived from the southwest. 'I descended into this space and aimed my torpedo at very short range at an easily identifiable cruiser of the *Pola* class.'[4] The attacking aircraft were met by a heavy barrage of anti-aircraft fire and the blinding effect of searchlights.

Lieutenant-Commander Bolt in the *Warspite* Swordfish K 8863 watched the attack from about five miles astern of the Italian fleet. He was frustrated he could not join in because his aircraft carried no bombs. 'The attack was most spectacular, the Italian fleet pouring out vast quan-tities of coloured tracer from their close-range weapons.'[5] Lieutenant Hopkins, the observer of Albacore 4A:

While waiting for the right light conditions we joined up with two Swordfish which had come out on their own from Crete. At first we thought they were Italian CR 42 bi-plane fighters and we spent some time dodging them. When we eventually went into attack from the dark side with the Italians silhouetted against the last glow of light in the west, we found we had been spotted at long range and were met with an impassable barrage of fire. We were forced to withdraw and split up and come in again individually from different angles.[6]

After the attack *Formidable*'s aircraft could not return to the carrier in the dark so they flew on to Suda Bay, where they landed between 21:00 and 23:00. 5A ran out of fuel and ditched in the sea; fortunately the destroyer *Juno* picked up the crew.

Whether it was Torrens-Spence or Lieutenant Kiggell with the second Maleme Swordfish who hit the cruiser *Pola* is hard to say, but it was likely to have been one of these aircraft. According to Torrens-Spence, 'It was subsequently confirmed by Italian prisoners-of-war that the *Pola* class cruiser was hit by a single aircraft attacking in the manner I described some minutes after the main attack.'[7]

Commander Bolt with Swordfish K 8863 was relieved of his shadowing role at 19:50 and told to return to Suda Bay. However they did not feel confident to land in Suda Bay, as it 'was steep [and] narrow, and with all the shore lights blacked out was not the sort of place to take liberties with on a very dark night.' The Swordfish put down in the sea at 21:25, PO Rice making a good landing, and they taxied five miles into the bay, identifying themselves to patrol boats with the aldis lamp. They had been airborne for eight hours, a remarkable flight.[8]

Back on board *Warspite*, Cunningham had some hard decisions to make; about 19:30 he received reports from the third strike of probable hits. Meanwhile the VALF reported enemy ships about nine miles from him to the northwest.

Now came the difficult moment of deciding what to do … it would be foolish not to make every effort to complete the *Vittorio Veneto*'s destruction. At the same time it appeared to us the Italian Admiral must have been fully aware of our position. He had numerous cruisers and destroyers in company … for attacks on the pursuing fleet. Some of my staff argued that it would be unwise to charge blindly after the retreating enemy with our three heavy ships, and the *Formidable* also on our hands, to run the risk of ships being crippled … I paid respectful attention to this opinion, and as the discussion happened to coincide with my time for dinner I told them I would have my evening meal and would see how I felt afterwards.[9]

After dinner Cunningham still felt confident that his fleet could perform successfully at night and was unwilling to let the enemy off the hook. Cunningham resolved to accept the risk of night action. If he delayed until daylight, the enemy would be under fighter cover and the Stukas would be waiting for the British Fleet.'[10] By 20:40 Cunningham had made up his mind to accept the risk of night action. He ordered the 2nd and 14th Destroyer Flotillas under the command of Captain Mack to find and attack the enemy; he would follow with the battle fleet.[11]

Geoffrey Barnard, the fleet gunnery officer, watched and spoke with Cunningham that night and he saw the 'well-known steely blue look in ABC's eye, and the staff had no doubt that there was going to be a party.' Cunningham seemed high on adrenalin, quite unlike the picture his own reminiscences paint of a calm, calculating man paying 'respectful attention' to his own staff. Barnard says he told them: 'You're a pack of yellow-livered skunks. I'll go and have my supper now and see after supper if my morale isn't higher than yours.'[12] One biography of Cunningham compares his going to dinner with Francis Drake calmly playing bowls. Of course there was little either commander could do at their respective times. But Cunningham hardly appears calm at any time like this, it was not his nature.[13]

On board *Vittorio Veneto* Admiral Iachino did appear calm. However he was still largely ignorant of the bigger picture, and might have been more agitated had he been better informed. Even after the dusk air attack it was some time before he was told that the heavy cruiser *Pola* had been hit. Before learning this he had been cheered by the fact that *Vittorio Veneto* could increase speed to 19 knots, and he revised his formation. Admiral Cattaneo's 1st Cruiser Division was ordered to take up station 5,000 yards ahead of the flagship, while Admiral Sansonetti's 3rd Division went 5,000 yards astern, both with their escorting destroyers. The 13th Destroyer Flotilla formed a close escort around *Vittorio Veneto*.

About this time a signal came in from Supermarina that D/F had learnt the enemy flagship had been transmitting to Alexandria at 17:45, only 40 miles off Cape Krio, at the south-western end of Crete. This put the British fleet much closer, 75 miles from *Vittorio Veneto*. However he though this message was based on interpretative error, and he was inclined to believe it was more than likely the VALF group of cruisers. Also Supermarina had not seemed unduly alarmed and had not made any recommendations.

However, soon more pressing concerns claimed Admiral Iachino's attention; *Vittorio Veneto* had picked up a signal from the cruiser *Zara* to *Pola* asking her condition. Obviously something was wrong. *Fiume* – which had been behind *Pola* – had seen her losing speed and then stopping altogether during the attack and had signalled *Zara*. A message, for some reason, that the flagship did not pick up. It soon became clear that *Pola* had been hit by a torpedo at the end of the attack and was in serious trouble. By this time she was several miles astern as the fleet had sailed on.

Admiral Iachino had little choice but to send a ship back to assess *Pola's* damage. With unknown British surface units at sea and possibly coming into the area he decided Admiral Cattaneo should return to *Pola's* aid with his division, *Zara*, *Fiume* and the 9th Destroyer Flotilla.

Admiral Cattaneo had intended to send back two destroyers. Iachino did not believe this was sufficient force to deal with the situation: to take off *Pola's* crew if necessary or to take the stricken cruiser in tow. By this time Cattaneo had a better idea of the state of *Pola* from her commander. She had been hit aft, one of her engine rooms was flooded and boilers 4, 5, 6 and 7, and she was requesting a tow.[14]

Notes

1 Schom, Alan, *Trafalgar: Countdown to Battle 1803–1805* p.307
2 Arthur, Max, *Lost Voices of the Royal Navy.*p.270
3 Bragadin, M.A. *The Italian Navy in World War II* p.91
4 Arthur, p.270–271
5 Pack, S.W.C. *The Battle of Matapan* p.93
6 Ibid p.95
7 Arthur, p.271
8 Pack, p.95–96
9 Cunningham A.B. *A Sailor's Odyssey* p.330
10 Navy Records Society. *The Cunningham Papers* p.238
11 Playfair, Major-General I.S.O. *The Mediterranean and Middle East Volume II* p.66
12 Pack, p.97–98
13 Pack, S.W.C. *Cunningham the Commander* p.143
14 Bragadin, p.90

16

Night Action 28/29 March

Admiral Iachino, although concerned, was confident that due to *Pola's* construction they would be able to salvage her. He still thought no British surface units were nearby. But he did signal Admiral Cattaneo: 'In case of encounter with superior forces, abandon *Pola.*' It was 21:06 when Cattaneo turned back with his ships toward *Pola.*[1]

Iachino informed Supermarina of his actions and that he intended to make for Taranto with the *Vittorio Veneto* and the 3rd Cruiser Division. About 20:45 he had altered course to 323° heading for the Gulf of Taranto at 19 knots.

On *Warspite* after Cunningham had finished dinner he ordered his destroyer force of eight ships

> ... to find and attack the enemy. We settled down to a steady pursuit with some doubts in our minds as to how the four destroyers remaining with the battle fleet would deal with the enemy destroyer attacks if the Italians decided to make them. At this stage the enemy fleet was estimated to be 33 miles ahead making good about fifteen knots.[2]

VALF had left the battle fleet about 19:00 with orders from Cunningham to find the *Vittorio Veneto.* Pridham-Wippell increased speed to 30 knots; his ships began to spread out in a search pattern seven miles wide. However they soon sighted ships ahead that seemed to be dropping back towards them. He ordered his ships to concentrate again and reduced speed. He feared the enemy might turn back to drive them off. About 19:40 he was only a dozen miles from the Italian fleet, and he informed the C-in-C he had sighted the enemy vessels. From his position they had seen the flashes of anti-aircraft fire and searchlights as the air attack had gone in.

About 20:15 Vice-Admiral Pridham-Wippell's flagship *Orion* received a report from the radar-equipped *Ajax* that she had plotted a ship six miles ahead. Further plots over the next few minutes revealed the vessel was stopped. About the same time *Gloucester* sighted a lone object low in the water. Further reports indicated a ship larger than a cruiser.

By 20:30 *Orion* was some way from the target, and the VALF informed Cunningham of the position and that it might be the damaged *Vittorio Veneto*. He decided to try and regain contact with the rest of the Italian fleet and leave the following battle fleet to deal with the mystery ship. However he never managed to regain contact.[3]

The news that an unknown ship was lying stopped reached Cunningham about 21:11. 'We went after the enemy's fleet, and altered course slightly to port to close the stopped ship.' *Warspite* led the battle fleet, followed in line astern by *Valiant*, *Formidable* and *Barham* about 600 yards apart. One mile to starboard were the destroyers *Stuart* and *Havock* and *Greyhound* and *Griffin* one mile to port.

> The *Warspite* was not fitted with radar, but at 10:10pm the *Valiant* reported that her instruments had picked up what was apparently the same ship 6 miles distant, which VALF had reported, on her port bow. She was a large ship. The *Valiant* gave her length as more than six hundred feet.[4]

Aboard the destroyer *Stuart* they found that night the sea

> ... as flat as a river. Above the masthead the stars hung countless in a luminous haze. The moon had not yet risen and the faint starlight seemed only to accentuate the darkness which fell wide and dense on all sides.[5]

On *Formidable*, after a hard day of flying operations many were trying to catch up on sleep. Pack had completed his weather chart before turning in; he had found the weather still fair, and a haze had reduced visibility to four or five miles. It was a dark night and the wind was light.[6]

The C-in-C changed course toward the radar target, hopes were running high it might be the *Vittorio Veneto*. The two screening destroyers on the port side were ordered to take station to starboard to clear the line of fire. The radar range plots steadily shrank.[7]

> Commodore [John] Edelsten, the new chief-of-staff had come to gain experience. And a quarter of an hour later at 10:25, when he was searching the horizon on the starboard bow with his glasses, he calmly reported that he saw two large cruisers with a smaller one ahead of them crossing the bows of the battle fleet, from starboard to port.[8]

They were rapidly identified as two *Zara* class 8-inch gun cruisers. Cunningham, even with the advantage of radar, had been surprised. Where he expected to find one ship he had found three. They were Admiral Cattaneo's ships *Zara* and *Fiume* and the destroyers looking for the *Pola.*

On the Italian ships they were completely unaware of the deadly danger; half their crews were stood down from battle stations in order to assist the *Pola*. On *Fiume*, towing cables were out and ready. Fatally, Cattaneo had at last found the stricken vessel. A red signal rocket had been sent up by *Pola* about 22:25; when her lookouts had seen dark shapes passing to the north these were in fact Cunningham's fleet.[9]

With the use of short range radio Admiral Cunningham ordered his battleships to change course to starboard, bringing them back into line ahead. All British ships by now knew the Italians were out there and close, and the crews were at action stations. *Formidable* drew out of line to starboard, being no use in this kind of action.

> In the dead silence, a silence that could almost be felt, one heard only the voices of the gun control personnel putting the guns onto the new target. One heard the orders repeated in the director tower behind and above the bridge.[10]

HMAS *Stuart*

> ... was directly astern of the line of battleships as they swept up. Looming out of the night six big ships rushed to meet them. From their course it seemed that the battleships hadn't been sighted. On *Warspite*, the leading British 15-incher, the huge barrels of her twin turrets trained smoothly round.[11]

The British ships moved steadily on, the range getting shorter. On the bridge of *Warspite*, according to signalman Donald Auffret, nerves were taut.

> [W]e were receiving the radar contacts and I can remember it got down to two-and-a-half miles range, almost abeam and still Cunningham didn't open fire and everybody was saying. 'For God's sake why doesn't he open fire?'[12]

The official history says the *Warspite*'s guns 'steadied on the second cruiser.' The range was down to 4,000 yards.[13]

> It must have been the fleet gunnery officer, Commander Geoffrey Barnard, who gave the final order to open fire. One heard the 'ting-ting-ting' of the firing gongs. Then came the great orange flash and the violent shudder as the six big guns bearing fired simultaneously. At the same instant the destroyer *Greyhound*, on the screen, switched her searchlight on to one of the enemy cruisers, showing her momentarily up as a silver-blue shape in the darkness. Our searchlights shone out with the first salvo, and provided full illumination for what was a ghastly sight.[14]

Inside *Warspite*'s X turret Roy Emmington was working on the guns but could see little.

> Salvoes shook the insides out of you so we were wondering what broadsides would do.
> We didn't have long to wonder, we got the orders to load both guns and we heard the breach workers shout 'Ready' and a few seconds later they fired ... A number of broadsides were fired that night ... It took us hours on the boys messdeck to unwind that night.[15]

It was 22:27 when *Warspite* opened fire, the range down to 3,000 yards. The ship that took the brunt of those first six 15-inch shells was *Fiume*. At least five hit her at this point blank range and she burst into flames just aft of the bridge back to the after turret, which was blown over the side, while others crashed into her just above the water line.

On board the *Stuart* they saw the *Fiume* 'dissolved into a mane of shearing flame. She heeled, stricken under the onslaught, transformed in a few

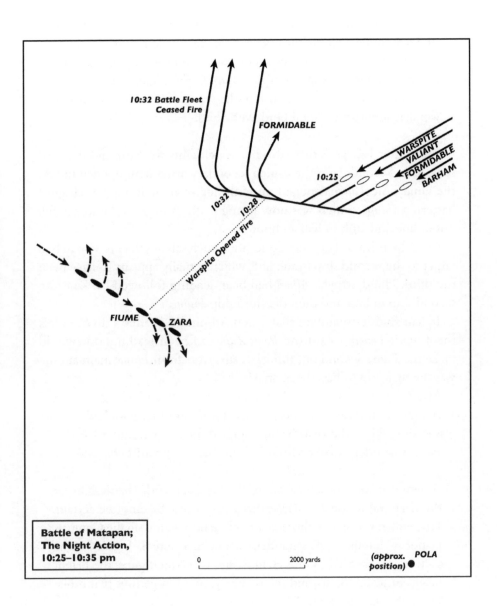

10:32 Battle Fleet
Ceased Fire

FORMIDABLE

WARSPITE
VALIANT
FORMIDABLE
BARHAM

10:25

10:32

10:28

Warspite Opened Fire

FIUME   ZARA

**Battle of Matapan;
The Night Action,
10:25–10:35 pm**

0   2000 yards

(approx.   POLA
position) ●

awful seconds from a proud fighting ship to a twisted tangle of iron.'[16] On the bridge of his flagship Cunningham was now largely a spectator.

> The Italians were quite unprepared. Their guns were trained fore and aft. They were helplessly shattered before they could put up any resistance. In the midst of all this there was a milder diversion. Captain Douglas Fisher, the captain of the *Warspite*, was a gunnery officer of note. When he saw the first salvo hit he was heard to say in a voice of wondering surprise. 'Good Lord. We've hit her.'[17]

Seconds after *Warspite*'s first salvo her searchlights were on, and she fired star-shells. Seconds later the 6-inch secondary armament opened fire. At the same time *Valiant* opened up with her 15-inch and 4.5-inch guns battering *Fiume*, which was now listing badly. A mass of flame, she fell out of line and sank in half an hour.

After the third of *Warspite*'s rapid fire 6-inch salvoes the crew switched target to the second ship in the line, which actually appears to have been the third. The destroyer *Alfieri* had been leading followed by *Zara*, the second ship in line, and then the third ship *Fiume*.

Italian sources maintain that when Admiral Cattaneo's division left the *Vittorio Veneto* to aid the *Pola*, *Zara* had been leading; this would make the *Fiume* second not third, but survivors from *Fiume* maintain she was the first ship to have been attacked.

About 22:15 Cattaneo had sent a destroyer ahead having seen a red Very light in the search for *Pola*. Thus *Alfieri* might have looked as if she was leading when the British ships opened fire a few minutes later.

Pack was rudely awoken from his slumbers on board *Formidable*.

> Whether it was the actual roar of the big guns of the battleships, or the alarm rattler on *Formidable* that I first heard, I cannot be certain. I remember rushing up the ladder to my action station on the Compass platform, donning jacket, muffler, steel helmet, anti-flash gear … The picture was dazzled by the vivid flashes of 15-inch guns, the bright beams of search lights, and the orange glow of huge fires that broke out in the ships under fire.[18]

By now the picture began to become confused, as Cunningham saw.

Our searchlights were still on, and just after 10:30 three Italian destroyers which had apparently been following their cruisers, were seen coming in on our port bow. They turned and one was seen to fire torpedoes, so the battle fleet was turned 90° to starboard to avoid them. Our destroyers were engaging and the whole party was inextricably mixed up.[19]

In the main action lasting only seven minutes *Warspite* had fired 40 rounds of 15-inch armour piercing shells and 44 of 6-inch high explosive shells. In the confusion, as Cunningham indicated, it was a wonder no ships had been hit or sunk by friendly fire.

To my horror I saw one of our destroyers the *Havock* , straddled by our fire, and in my mind wrote her off as a loss. The *Formidable* also had an escape. When action was joined she hauled out to starboard at full speed, a night battle being no place for a carrier.

When she was about five miles away she was caught in the beam of the *Warspite's* searchlight sweeping on the disengaged side in case further enemy ships were present.

We heard the 6-inch control officer of the starboard battery get his guns on to her, and were only just in time to stop him from opening fire.[20]

On the blazing and listing *Fiume* the captain ordered the crew to abandon ship at 23:15. *Zara* was in as bad a shape; the flames were leaping as high as her masts and the crew was also ordered to abandon ship, but she was sinking slowly so the second-in-command went below to set charges to blow her up. At 00:30 she blew up taking Admiral Cattaneo and many others on board down with her.

The destroyer *Alfieri* had been hit many times and had dozens of casualties. They still managed to fire some torpedoes, but they all missed, probably because of the list of the damaged ship. Finally her commander made the order to abandon ship. On the destroyer *Carducci* the crew were unable to bring the fires under control; the commander scuttled the ship, going down with her.

The *Oriani*, although damaged, managed to make it home as did the *Gioberti*, the only ship under Cattaneo's command that was undamaged. It was probably the *Gioberti's* brave torpedo attack on the British battleships that forced the latter to turn away.[21]

At 22:40 Admiral Cunningham had ordered his destroyers to finish off the cruisers, while the battle fleet withdrew to the north. The *Stuart* used all her torpedoes attacking two ships, while the *Havock* could find no target.

About 23:00 *Stuart* got in a fire fight with two enemies she thought were cruisers; in fact they were destroyers, and later Captain Waller was able to identify one as a *Grecale* class destroyer. One was *Oriani*, the two ships passing within 150 yards of each other. *Greyhound* and *Griffin* also got involved in the melee; they believed that they scored several hits on an enemy cruiser, and chased some enemy destroyers for some miles, until they were ordered to withdraw.

> Just after 11am I made a signal ordering all forces not engaged in sinking the enemy to withdraw to the north-eastward. The objects of what I now consider to have been an ill-considered signal were to give our destroyers who were mopping up a free hand to attack any sizeable ship they saw and to facilitate the assembly of the fleet next morning. The message was qualified by an order to Captain Mack, and his eight destroyers of the striking force, now some twenty miles ahead, not to withdraw until he attacked. However, it had the unfortunate effect of causing Vice-Admiral Pridham-Wippell to cease his efforts to gain touch with the *Vittorio Veneto*.[22]

Notes
1 Bragadin, M.A. *The Italian Navy in World War II* p.92
2 Cunningham, A.B. *A Sailor's Odyssey* p.330
3 Playfair, Major-General I.S.O. *The Mediterranean and Middle East Volume II* p.67
4 Cunningham, p.331
5 HMAS *Stuart*. *www.diggerhistory.aus*
6 Pack, S.W.C. *The Battle of Matapan* p.112
7 Playfair, p.67
8 Cunningham, p.331
9 Bragadin, p.93–94
10 Cunningham, p.332
11 HMAS *Stuart*. *www.diggerhistory.aus*
12 Ballantyne, Iain, *Warspite* p.123
13 Playfair, p.67
14 Cunningham p.332
15 Coward, Commander R.B. *Battleship at War* p.173
16 HMAS *Stuart*. www.diggerhistory.aus
17 Cunningham, p.332
18 Pack, p.113

19 Cunningham, p.332–333
20 Ibid p.333
21 Bragadin, p.94–95
22 Cunningham, p.333

17

The Italian Cruisers

At 22:27 when *Warspite* opened fire, the Italian cruisers were taken completely by surprise and were unprepared for action. *Pola* had been hit by a Swordfish torpedo at 19:50 during the dusk attack. At the time she was the middle ship of the 1st Cruiser Division on the starboard side of the centre group around the *Vittorio Veneto*. At that moment Captain De Pisa had slowed his ship as he was closing on *Zara* ahead. The force of the torpedo explosion struck the no 3 boiler room and the port engine, the torpedo exploding under the ship, resulting in a complete loss of power. All electrical power was gone as well, but the ship was in no immediate danger of sinking. Captain De Pisa tried to raise steam but all his boilers were damaged. The 1st Cruiser Division and 9th Destroyer Flotilla turned back to find *Pola* at 21:06. They were near *Pola* when they met the British.

Cattaneo and his staff were quite confident about their security; the Admiral believed the British battle fleet was still in Alexandria. The crews of *Zara* and *Fiume* were making ready to take *Pola* in tow. He had received the Supermarina report of 17:45 that a British force had been 75 miles astern of *Vittorio Veneto*, but like Iachino he seemed unconcerned by it.

Pola's captain, seeing dark shapes passing in the distance but with no power, ordered a red Very light fired. The signal was seen on *Zara*. Captain L. Corsi of the flagship was heard to say by Sub-Lieutenant Giorgi Parodi: 'There's the *Pola*. Is that our recognition signal?' Parodi told him it was not.

It was then they were bathed in light by *Greyhound's* searchlight followed rapidly by the firing of *Warspite's* guns. At first Corsi thought *Pola* was firing on them. *Fiume*, ahead, burst into flames and they soon realised the size of the guns that were firing. Alarms and action stations were sounded. Corsi ordered an increase in speed and the helm put hard to starboard. The *Zara* herself was soon hit and in flames. The first turret, A turret, was hit and exploded. Another shell passed under the bridge wrecking all communications.

Parodi was ordered below to stop the engines, so the crew could abandon ship. For two hours the crew had tried to save the ship and care for the wounded. According to Parodi, Admiral Cattaneo ordered the *Zara* scuttled. 'The crew of *Zara* does not surrender. I have given orders to sink the ship,' he was heard to say.

Parodi later stated that 'the water was very cold' as he swam away from the ship; about 100 metres out he heard and felt the first internal explosions of the charges that blew out the ship's bottom. A short while later the bow magazine exploded.

> When the flames died down the *Zara* seemed to be trying to lift herself out of the water. Then she began to turn over. A few minutes later there came a succession of huge waves ... Then all was dark.[1]

The early destruction of *Zara*'s electrical systems by *Warspite*'s first salvo made it impossible to return fire. Also the Italians' night fighting techniques were extremely undeveloped; the main 8-inch guns were ineffective at night as they did not have flashless charges, thus the gunlayers would be blinded making accurate fire impossible. The secondary 3.9-inch guns could have been used but lacked electrical power.

The Italians were staggered by the British ability to fight so intensively at night. Admiral Cunningham found the Italian night-fighting hopelessly out of date, on a par with that of the British during the First World War, and the night action as 'more like murder than anything else'.[2]

Within minutes of *Fiume* being hit she stopped and was unable to return fire for the same reasons as *Zara*. A raging fire took hold around the after turret, and Captain G. Giorg and his crew tried to bring the fire under control. Finding it impossible, all ready to use ammunition was thrown over the side. The ship soon began listing alarmingly and the captain ordered the crew to abandon ship. Most of the rafts were put into the sea. *Fiume* capsized and sank by the stern about 23:15.

Admiral Iachino felt that Cattaneo had made a serious error by steaming in line ahead and too close together. His destroyers should have been fanned out ahead of the cruisers or at some distance on either flank. This would have aided in the search for *Pola* and was in standing orders. As we have seen, only one destroyer was ahead. Had they been in the correct formation the cruisers would have received some warning of the presence of British heavy units.[3]

On board the destroyer *Alfieri*, Sub-Lieutenant Vito Sansonetti, son of Admiral Sansonetti, wrote of what he saw. He was entering the bridge when

> I suddenly saw an enormous flame a few hundred metres in front of the bows, which grew larger on the starboard side. It seemed higher than 50 metres and about 100 metres wide. Suddenly, I heard the sound of explosions. I ran out and saw large pieces flying through the air from the cruiser which had been hit.

Alfieri was soon hit, taking most of the first salvoes from *Barham*.

> Our speed slackened as we described a circle. In the meantime I had seen many hits on the cruiser, which must have been the *Fiume*, and saw many shells fall into the sea near us.

Sansonetti made his way to the torpedo tubes: 'The crews were at their posts and asking for orders. I told them not to worry and prepare for firing.' They were soon in action against the British destroyers.

'The ship was heeling over quite a bit to starboard and the enemy destroyer passed not more than 200 metres away.' Sansonetti managed to fire some of the torpedoes but because *Alfieri* was listing badly had little hope of hitting anything. 'The torpedo men remained at their posts and carried out all orders with discipline and calm, although shells were falling all around and fragments had killed and wounded many of them.' Soon the captain ordered abandon ship, and after he had seen his men were away Sansonetti jumped over the side. The *Alfieri* was the only Italian ship to offer any resistance, sinking about 23:30.[4]

About 23:00 Captain Waller of the destroyer *Stuart* had lost touch with the Italians.

> I had also lost touch with the *Havock* and was feeling somewhat alone. I worked round to the north-east. At 11.30am a cruiser [destroyer] was

sighted to the NNE and engaged. A feeble fire was returned. We got several hits on this cruiser and started a fire on board her. She ceased fire and I continued retirement to the north-east.[5]

Havock was not far away, moving about the burning and sinking Italian ships, on which she used her remaining torpedoes. She then turned north to comply with Cunningham's signal, firing star shells to finally check the area. To her commander's surprise they revealed a large ship which appeared undamaged and was stopped. They thought it a battleship, but it was the ship that had caused the night action, the ill-fated *Pola*.

Continuing northeast putting on speed *Havock* opened fire on the ship with little effect and sent a signal that she had engaged a *Vittorio Veneto* class battleship at about 23:45. Shortly after midnight the commander of *Havock*, Lieutenant G.R.G. Watkins, corrected his first signal. Having now identified the ship as an 8-inch gun cruiser, and given its position, he advised that he was turning about to shadow the vessel, and that he had no more torpedoes.

Since 21:00 the eight destroyers under Captain Mack in the *Jervis* had been heading westward at full speed in pursuit of the enemy fleet, which unknown to him had altered course to the northwest and increased speed. About 23:00 he thought he might be ten miles to the northwest having overtaken the enemy. However at that time he was 25 miles south of, and behind, the main group of Italian ships. At 00:30 Mack intercepted *Havock*'s signal about finding a battleship; he immediately turned back with both flotillas, only to hear later that it was a heavy cruiser. Mack decided to continue on his course to the firm sighting rather than chasing shadows, and at 02:00 he saw searchlights ahead.[6]

Cunningham wrote in his official report:

> The mistake in the *Havock*'s signal did not actually bring about any ill effect, since the flotillas had by then missed the *Vittorio Veneto* and did useful work in polishing off the damaged cruiser.[7]

Greyhound and *Griffin* were also complying with Cunningham's order, when they picked up *Havock*'s signal and they turned back to the south. At 00:40 *Greyhound* signalled that she had found *Pola* stopped on an even keel but low in the water; her guns were lying fore and aft, and her ensign was still flying.

On *Pola* they had been spectators to the night's events swirling around them but powerless to do anything. The cruiser had no power to use her guns or to move. Any minute they had expected British ships to come in and attack them, so her commander Captain M. De Pisa reluctantly ordered the sea valves opened and the crew to abandon ship.

British ships passed them several times but seemed unaware of their presence. It was not until after midnight that *Havock* sighted her and then pulled away. About 01:10 destroyers came back, fired a few shells and pulled away again.

Pola was sinking slowly and because of the cold her crew started to get back on board. De Pisa stopped the scuttling to give his men somewhere to wait for rescue. About 03:00, several British destroyers turned up (Mack's Command); by now the water was up to *Pola*'s decks.

Jervis came alongside and took off 258 survivors, the last being De Pisa. After fifteen minutes *Jervis* cast off from the stricken cruiser and fired a torpedo into her and she settled slowly. *Nubian* fired another torpedo and *Pola* blew up and sank at 04:03, the final act of destruction in the Battle of Matapan.[8]

According to Cunningham, when the British destroyers *Havock*, *Greyhound*, *Griffin* and Captain Mack's flotillas arrived, the *Pola* was

... in a state of indescribable confusion. Panic stricken men were leaping over the side. On the crowded quarterdeck, littered with clothing, personal belongings and bottles, many of the sailors were drunk. There was no order or discipline of any sort, and the officers were powerless to enforce it.[9]

Commander Bragadin was convinced that this did not happen. 'The version put out at the time by the British propaganda service, and repeated also by Admiral Cunningham, about the "panic and confusion" on board the *Pola* is entirely without foundation.'[10]

Commander Walter Scott of the *Jervis* was an eyewitness to events. 'The 257 Italian ratings filed on board in an orderly fashion over a brow hastily put out, and were followed by the commander and captain of *Pola*.'

At this time a boarding party went on the cruiser and came back with

... a story of chaos on board. The officers' cabins had been looted by the ship's company of the *Pola*, and empty Chianti bottles lay everywhere. Verification of this came when a number of prisoners showed unmistakable signs of inebriation.[11]

The British destroyers continued to pick up survivors prior to the regrouping of the fleet.

Notes
1 Ufficio Storcio Marina Militare. *G. Parodi narrative*
2 Navy Records Society, *The Cunningham Papers Vol.1* p.239
3 Seth, Ronald, *Two Fleets Surprised: The Battle of Cape Matapan* p.150
4 Ufficio Storcio Marina Militare. *V. Sansonetti narrative*
5 PRO, Captain Waller Narrative HMAS *Stuart*
6 Playfair, Major-General I.S.O. *The Mediterranean and Middle East Volume II* p.68
7 Naval Records Society p.312
8 Bragadin, M.A. *The Italian Navy in World War II* p.94–95
9 Cunningham, A.B. *A Sailor's Odyssey* p.333–334
10 Bragadin, p.95
11 Pack, S.W.C. *The Battle of Matapan* p.134

18

29 March

At 04:30 *Formidable* flew off four aircraft to conduct searches; only a small number of rafts and survivors were seen. There was no sign of the battleship *Vittorio Veneto* or any Italian ships.

The British fleet assembled at 07:00. Except for one Swordfish missing from *Formidable,* none had casualties or damage. Admiral Cunningham was glad of this as he had been convinced *Warspite* had sunk one of his own destroyers in the melee. '[W]e eagerly counted them. To our inexpressible relief all twelve destroyers were present.'[1]

It was a fine morning as the fleet steamed back to the scene of the battle on a mercy mission. The area was covered by a film of oil and dotted with boats, rafts, and wreckage and floating corpses. In all, including the men taken off *Pola* during the night, 900 were rescued although some died later. A further 110 were picked up by a Greek destroyer flotilla, which had failed to join in the action owing to a mistake in the ciphering of orders.[2]

However the fleet soon drew the attention of some German JU 88 bombers who attacked the ships; they were barely 100 miles west of Crete and 50 miles southwest of Cape Matapan. The fleet was compelled to withdraw eastwards leaving hundreds of men still in the water. An aircraft was flown off *Formidable* with a message it took to Suda Bay for transmission to Malta where it was to be broadcast to the Chief of the Italian naval staff. It gave the position of the survivors still in the water. The Italian hospital ship *Gradisca* picked up a further 160 men over two days. Overall the Italians had suffered some 2,400 casualties.

On the return to Alexandria, *Formidable* kept her fighter flying patrols above the fleet. They were able to deal with twelve JU 88s who attacked the fleet at 15:30. Four near misses shook *Formidable*– as always the carrier was the first target – but there was no damage. Two of the JU 88s were shot down. Pack saw one

> ... come lower and lower, until with a great white splash he crashed into the sea to port, and instantly disappeared. The bombing from the first six had been alarmingly accurate. The last four of the formation, however, had been forced to drop their bombs hurriedly, when attacked by *Formidable*'s fighters.[3]

The fleet arrived at Alexandria at 17:30 on a pleasant spring evening.

Surgeon-Commander Sorley wrote home from Alexandria on 30 March 1941 with obvious elation.

> The whole episode is very heartening and yesterday morning when the total enemy damage was announced to us by the C-in-C, the sense of jubilation amongst our officers and men was good to see. One felt one had been privileged to be in a force that had struck a great blow at the enemies of the King and one was flushed with the knowledge of our naval power and courage. For remember that the whole Italian force was numerically superior to ours, but as we expected, their ships preferred to run away; but not before we could inflict terrible blows. If their force had stayed to fight, this would have been another Trafalgar; as it is, we doubt if the Italian fleet will dare to challenge us again.[4]

On the Italian side, there was appprehension and then terrible confirmation. Admiral Iachino on the bridge of *Vittorio Veneto*, had seen the Very lights astern thinking Admiral Cattaneo must be in action about 22:30. The distance was 40 miles. He signalled *Zara* but there was no reply. Then vivid flashes began lighting the sky to the southeast and they could hear the boom of guns. He knew they could not be Italian 8-inch guns. He felt Cattaneo must have come across the British cruisers.[5]

The flagship tried signalling all the ships of Cattaneo's command, even the destroyers, but no reply came in. With *Vittorio Veneto* damaged, Iachino did not even consider turning back into the unknown.

Then at 05:00 a signal came in from the destroyer *Gioberti* which said; 'Disengaged from 1st Naval Squadron, ships of flotilla do not reply. Having searched again for enemy have reached the limit of my endurance' and was proceeding to Augusta. This of course did little to allay Iachino's anxiety but there was little he could do but steam on toward Taranto.

At 06:00 five JU 88s arrived over the fleet from Sicily and took station. An hour later the destroyer *Oriani* signalled that British fire had damaged one of her engines and she was heading for Augusta. Two hours later she signalled again; speed reduced she was limping asking for a tow. Admiral Iachino sent the destroyers *Maestrale* and *Libeccio* to bring in *Oriani*; he asked Supermarina to arrange air cover for them.

Vittorio Veneto reached Taranto at 15:00 on 29 March without further incident; the disastrous Operation *Gaudo* was over.

Notes

1   Cunningham, A.B. *A Sailor's Odyssey* p.334
2   Ibid p.334
3   Pack, S.W.C. *The Battle of Matapan* p.141
4   BBC World War II archives. Surgeon–Commander E.R. Sorley
5   Bragadin, M.A. *The Italian Navy in World War II* p.96

Part Three

Conclusions

There is little doubt that the rough handling given the enemy on this occasion served us in good stead during the subsequent evacuations of Greece and Crete. Much of these later operations may be said to have been conducted under the cover of the Battle of Matapan.[1]

Admiral Cunningham

19

Effects of Matapan

Commander Bragadin:

> Let us pass now to some conclusions about this affair. The whole opera-
> tion hinged entirely upon three prerequisites which failed to materialise.
> From the moment when the Sunderland sighted the 3rd Division off
> Sicily, surprise was lacking. The political motive which made it impos-
> sible to call off the operation has already been noted. There was no
> effective air reconnaissance. The scarce and inaccurate reports which
> were received did not permit those at Italian headquarters to form a
> really clear picture of the situation at sea, nor did reconnaissance ever
> reveal the vital information that the entire Mediterranean Fleet out of
> Alexandria was but a short distance away from the Italian formation.
> The ineffectiveness of this air reconnaissance was further aggravated
> by errors in the use of radio frequencies on the part of Italian air crews,
> with the result that some reports came through very late.[2]

A few days after the battle, Admiral Iachino was summoned to appear
before Mussolini in Rome; the C-in-C fleet had already received a cool
reception from the Naval High Command. It must have been with the
trepidation of a sacrificial lamb that he arrived at the *Palazzo Venezia*.
Built for the Venetian Pope Paul II in the mid-fifteenth century and for
many years the embassy of the Venetian Republic, in 1941 it was the seat
of the Fascist Government. Mussolini's offices were in the vast *Sala del
Moppamondo*, and he made many of his most famous speeches from the
small balcony facing onto the piazza proper.

Iachino was accompanied by the Chief of the Naval Staff, Admiral Riccardi. He was made to wait in an anteroom while the C-N-S saw Mussolini, which must have done little for Iachino's nerves.

Presently the fleet C-in-C was ushered into the vast room. Mussolini had his marble desk at the far end, thus the visitor had a long walk under his gaze. *Il Duce* felt it gave him the advantage over any guest. General Guzzoni, Vice-Chief of the General Staff and Admiral Riccardi were there. Mussolini was stood in the centre behind the desk dressed in civilian clothes.

Iachino came to a halt before the desk at attention, saluted and waited. Mussolini seemed anything but grim to him. When he spoke he was calm and asked Iachino to tell him what had happened during Operation *Gaudo*. The Admiral knew *Il Duce* must already know in detail what had happened, so he kept his report short. Mussolini questioned the wisdom of sending the 1st Cruiser Division back to aid the *Pola*, asking that surely two destroyers would have been enough; obviously this point had been raised with Riccardi beforehand. The C-in-C gave his reply that two destroyers could have only sunk the *Pola*, whereas he was trying to save the ship. At first Mussolini seemed unconvinced by the answer, but appeared to change his mind on pressing the point further. He began to pace up and down behind his desk, and after a short while began to speak.

Iachino, he said, had carried out a necessary operation mainly for political reasons, a thankless task. However he believed it would have a good effect on morale taking the fight to the British in the eastern Mediterranean, a sphere they called their own. It had begun under favourable conditions, and had failed mainly through a complete lack of co-operation from the air forces. All the aircraft in the air in the main area of operations had belonged to the enemy.

> Your ships were like a blind giant who is suddenly attacked by a number of men with good eyesight and armed with dangerous weapons. It is a serious matter, and imposes on us the solution of a problem of the utmost urgency.[3]

Mussolini's analysis was entirely correct, although it was unfortunate for the Regia Marina that he had not come to this conclusion earlier, rather than continually swallowing the Regia Aeronautica's line. However, it should be noted that 'the tactical success of Admiral Cunningham was due mainly to the use of radar, something still unknown to the Italians.' Also added to this should be the paralysis that gripped Admiral Cattaneo's command in regard to night fighting.[4]

Mussolini stopped pacing, and declared naval operations should not be conducted in future in enemy waters without air reconnaissance and fighter cover. Fighter aircraft had limited endurance, therefore,

> It is necessary, in short, for naval forces at sea to be always accompanied by at least one carrier. The problem is already being studied. I have given orders to my Chief of General Staff to make arrangements immediately for the construction of a carrier, and I am sure that we shall have it soon, probably within a year.

In the meantime naval operations would be confined to western waters controlled by Italian aircraft.

Leaving the *Palazzo Venezia*, Iachino was naturally pleased his actions had been largely vindicated, but doubtful the navy would ever receive carriers. In this he was to be proved right.[5]

With Mussolini's backing,

> ... it was immediately decided to transform the transatlantic liner *Roma* into an aircraft carrier, which would be called the *Aquila*. Following this decision, a similar conversion was initiated on the transatlantic liner *Augustus* which was to become the aircraft carrier *Sparviero*.

However the work went slowly; by the armistice of September 1943 *Aquila* was virtually finished but had no aircraft. The *Sparviero* still needed months of work.[6]

Admiral Iachino remained C-in-C of the Italian battle fleet until 1942 when he took up a post in the Ministry of Marine.

In his report on Matapan Cunningham wrote:

> The results of the action cannot be viewed with entire satisfaction, since the damaged *Vittorio Veneto* was allowed to escape. The failure of the cruisers and destroyers to make contact with her during the night was unlucky and is much to be regretted.[7]

Admiral Cunningham is rightly credited with the victories at Taranto and Matapan. However the first at Taranto, although he gave the green light and encouraged those involved, was the result of planning by many officers of the Fleet Air Arm, going back to the carrier *Glorious* in 1935 and the commander-in-chief at the time Admiral Sir William Wordsworth Fisher. It also owed much to the time spent by the fleet air arm pilots practising and perfecting night flying techniques. It must also be remembered that Cunningham was the product of the 'big gun' era and came to a grudging recognition of the part fliers were to play, which matured over the years.

Cunningham had a natural grasp of new ideas, even if he hankered after a great fleet action. It was he who had stopped the carrier falling out of line for landing and takeoff of aircraft, which had become a habit for some flag officers, who resented the whole fleet having to change direction just for flying operations. Cunningham felt the carriers were vulnerable and needed the anti-aircraft support of heavy units, thus the entire fleet took part in the carrier's manoeuvre, both parts lending support to one another. This became standard practice especially in the Pacific, where in one action, when battleships and cruisers were busy supplying bombardment support for landings, the Allied carrier fleet suffered in a heavy Kamikaze attack.[8]

At Matapan, Cunningham commanded the first fleet action involving air power – both carrier- and land-based. Admiral Iachino was amazed that the British could co-ordinate torpedo and bomber attacks so well. Indeed Cunningham was the architect of this and pulled it off to a degree, in some ways more by luck than judgement, but nevertheless it was his aim and it came off resulting in the damage to *Vittorio Veneto*.

The damage to the heavy cruiser *Pola* must be as much to the credit of Lieutenant Torrens-Spence and 815 Squadron Fleet Air Arm, with the aircraft that had served on *Illustrious*, who flew from Greece and Crete with great skill just to get into the battle.

In the night action, Cunningham used his battleships more like destroyers with devastating effect, realising he could not risk waiting until daylight when they would be closer to Italy and enemy air power. Luck was on his side, as his battle fleet arrived at the same time as the Italian 1st Cruiser Division looking for *Pola*, and he had the all-seeing eye of radar, although *Valiant's* radar set picked up the *Pola* but not the other cruisers. Cunningham wanted to bring on a pell-mell battle but admits himself that in such an action,

Instant and momentous decisions have to be made in a matter of seconds. With fast-moving ships at close quarters and the roar of heavy gunfire in night action at sea, clear thinking is not easy. In no other circumstances than in night action at sea does the fog of war so completely descend to blind one to a true realisation of what is happening.[9]

Cunningham admits his order of 23:00 for 'all forces not engaged to withdraw to the north eastward' was ill-considered, as it meant Vice-Admiral Pridham-Wippell gave up the chase of *Vittorio Veneto* when his cruisers were the closest British ships, whereas Captain Mack and his eight destroyers were the only ships ordered not to withdraw until they attacked. However, unknown to Cunningham and Mack the latter had already missed *Vittorio Veneto* and the first *Havock* signal brought Mack back to the cruisers thinking they had found a battleship as well. Neither Cunningham nor Captain Philip Mack can really be criticised for either action.[10]

Admiral Cunningham's battles are often compared to Horatio Nelson's victories. The first date for the raid on Taranto was to have been 21 October, Trafalgar Day; however as we know for various reasons Operation *Judgement* was postponed until the night of 11 November 1940. Taranto is often compared to Nelson's battles at the Nile and Copenhagen, where he attacked enemy fleets in their own anchorages. The Nile battle against the French fleet of 1 August 1798 at Aboukir Bay, started at dusk and continued into darkness. The Battle of Copenhagen on 2 April 1801 is perhaps a better comparison, when Nelson sent his frigates into the harbour. Although it took place in daylight, the anchorage has similarities to Taranto, and the Danish fleet had persistently refused to put to sea to face the Royal Navy. There the similarities end, other than for Cunningham's determination, like Nelson's 'to get at the enemy'.[11]

The comparison between Matapan and Trafalgar is rather stronger. Both Admirals wanted to bring on a pell-mell battle, Nelson from the very beginning; Cunningham came to that conclusion by charging after the enemy with his battleships. Both used innovative tactics, although Cunningham's were rather newer to him than were Nelson's. The result of both battles crippled enemy sea power for many months, years in the case of Nelson.

General Eisenhower saw Cunningham as

... the Nelsonian type who believed ships went to sea in order to find and destroy the enemy. The degree of affection in which he was held by all, both British and American, was nothing short of remarkable.[12]

Admiral Iachino felt Cunningham was a 'generous' and 'chivalrous opponent,' particularly in his actions to try and save as many Italian sailors as possible on 29 March.[13] However there is another school of thought that saw him as an 'intolerant dinosaur', with no real grasp of air power and rather dismissive of other technical advances. Many feel he should have opposed the defence of Crete more vigorously, which caused heavy losses to the Mediterranean Fleet. In his own papers he wrote:

> The Greek odyssey was but a prologue to the Navy's greatest trial and tragedy in the Mediterranean, the battle for Crete, which took place three weeks after the final evacuation from Greece. If the Greek expedition was an unavoidable moral and diplomatic commitment, the decision to hold Crete was essentially a military one.[14]

Cunningham did not seem to have grasped his misuse of *Illustrious* earlier in the war, for again he sent a vulnerable carrier with an exhausted air group into the thick of the battle.

On 26 May, Pridham-Wippell led a force including *Formidable* into the Aegean to attack the Scarpanto aerodrome on Rhodes. One of the most dangerous of enemy airfields, it lay beyond the range of any land-based British fighters. *Formidable* had only a few serviceable aircraft left; just two Fulmars and six Albacores were able to attack Scarpanto, doing minimal damage. On the return the carrier was attacked by 25 JU 88s, escorted by ME 110s. Four Fulmars put up a valiant defence but *Formidable* was hit twice and damaged by near misses. Like *Illustrious* she would spend months in the US being repaired.

The Cunningham papers state: 'The decision to employ the carrier on this mission when it was known that both her striking force and, more particularly, her fighter squadrons were so weak is beyond comprehension.'

Formidable should have been kept well clear of the battle. Cunningham may have been distracted by the battle for Crete, overly influenced perhaps by Fleet Air Arm advisors, but surely the *Illustrious* experience must have resonated with him.

He must have been aware that, as Pound [Admiral Sir Dudley Pound] pointed out the cupboard was virtually bare. One senses a note of reproach in Pound's comment that to send him another carrier 'would be a sheer waste'.[15]

Churchill and the War Cabinet wanted Crete defended. The British Army felt if the Germans could be restricted to an air assault then they could hold Crete. So Cunningham and his hard working fleet were put on the spot.

After Matapan the Mediterranean Fleet had a busy period. On 18 April it bombarded the biggest Italian air base at Tripoli in North Africa. The fleet returned from that operation to begin the evacuation of the army from the shores of Greece. After that was done it was back into the central Mediterranean within easy reach of the Luftwaffe, to escort the 'Tiger' convoy bearing much needed weapons and munitions for the British Army and RAF. Losses were small: one merchant ship sunk, but 238 tanks and 43 cased Hurricane fighters were brought safely to Egypt. Good work by British fighters, both land- and carrier-based and heavy anti-aircraft fire from warships did much to protect the convoy. The weather, thick and cloudy, was on the British side. The fleet also received reinforcements coming through with this convoy in the shape of the modernised battleship *Queen Elizabeth* and the cruisers *Naiad* and *Fiji*. The Admiralty felt it was a 'memorable achievement'.[16]

Cunningham at this point does not seem to have been over confident:

Unfortunately the apparent ease with which the convoy was brought through from end to end of the Mediterranean caused many false conclusions to be drawn at home, and I think made some people think that we were exaggerating the dangers and difficulties of running con-voys and operations of any sort in the face of the vigorous action of the Luftwaffe. Before long the dismal truth was painfully to be brought home to them.[17]

Churchill had no doubts Crete should be held, as he informed the Army C-in-C General Sir Archibold Wavell on 17 April.

Crete must be held ... and you should provide for this in the redis-tribution of your forces ... It is important that strong elements of the

Greek Army should establish themselves in Crete together with the King and Government.

He was quick to interfere with the Admiralty, questioning Cunningham on the wisdom of defending Crete.

You are giving him the strongest lead to abandon Crete. I thought our view was that Crete should be held at all reasonable cost.

General Wavell sent General 'Jumbo' Wilson to Crete to assess the situation, the latter reaching the island on 27 April. He soon reported that, unless all three services were 'prepared to face the strain of maintaining adequate forces up to strength, the holding of the island was a dangerous commitment, and a decision on the matter must be taken at once.' This was really pointed at the RAF, who had far too few fighter aircraft available for the island's defence, having lost over 200 fighter aircraft in the defence of Greece that could not be rapidly replaced. However Churchill insisted 'The Island must be stubbornly defended.'[18]

Cunningham wrote:

It was the general opinion that the island could be held against airborne only. However it was expected that the enemy might also attempt a seaborne landing in support.

The repulse of this latter assault stood out as the Navy's main function and it was with this end in view that we made our dispositions.

It appears that the Ultra decodes, so vital in the victory at Matapan, may have made the British over-confident in the defence of Crete. On 6 May the Bletchley Park code breakers identified the probable date of completion of German preparations as 17 May and had the complete final operation orders for the execution of the assault. Churchill was cock-a-hoop about this, considering the information priceless.

The German invasion was given the codename 'Scorcher' by the British, and Crete became 'Colorado'. The German codename for the invasion was Operation *Mercury*.

The Chiefs of Staff certainly did discuss the Ultra Enigma evidence. All would have been well aware of the part Ultra had played in

Cunningham's victory at Matapan, but things were not so clear cut with regards to Crete. There were also concerns about Iraq, Cyprus and Syria.

Churchill felt this gave them a winning hand. They would be able to trap the German paratroops on Crete, cutting them off from the sea with no hope of retreat or reinforcement, forcing them to surrender. It was this vision that encouraged Churchill's deep personal interest in the defence of Crete.

After the loss of Crete, in a seemingly rapid twelve days a 'searching investigation' at the time could not take place because it would inevitably have breached security by revealing the role of Ultra.[19] Cunningham wrote in a dispatch:

> That the fleet suffered disastrously in this encounter with the unhampered German Air Force is evident, but it has to be remembered on the credit side that the Navy's duty was achieved and no enemy ship, whether warship or transport, succeeded in reaching Crete or intervening in the battle during those critical days. Nor should the losses sustained blind one to the magnificent courage and endurance that was displayed throughout. I have never felt prouder of the Mediterranean Fleet than at the close of these particular operations, except perhaps, at the fashion in which it faced up to the even greater strain which was so soon to be imposed upon it.[20]

The Royal Navy's success failed to tip the balance in Crete. The official history observed:

> It is perhaps fairer to conclude that, whereas the Germans had the strength to off-set bad intelligence, the British, whether from weakness or for other reasons, were not in a position to make better use of the intelligence service that was at last getting into its stride.[21]

The loss of Crete was down to the lack of British air cover, anti-aircraft guns, transport and poor communications on the ground. The troops, tired from the retreat from Greece, fought well. General Freyberg made mistakes; Brigadier Keith Stewart believed that Freyberg made 'a balls' of the defence. But he faced impossible conditions; Callum MacDonald says in his history of the battle that 'It is doubtful if any other general could have done better.'[22]

At Matapan, Cunningham had the advantage of Ultra intelligence plus the Fleet Air Arm, radar, and the technical ability of his fleet to fight at night. There was little he could do about the decision to defend Crete which was driven by Winston's Churchill's belief they could not lose with Ultra intelligence.[23]

At Matapan, Cunningham did well in co-ordinating air strikes and deciding to pursue the enemy fleet at night, against the advice of some of his staff. There is some truth in the accusation that he did not fully understand the use of carriers or air matters, but that was true of several commanders in other fleets. Above all, Cunningham was a lucky commander. As Napoleon is reputed to have said, 'give me a lucky general every time.'

Notes
 1 Navy Records Society, *The Cunningham Papers Volume I* p.313
 2 Bragadin, M.A. *The Italian Navy in World War II* p.96–97
 3 Iachino, Admiral Angelo, *Gaudo and Matapan* p.163–165
 4 Bragadin, p.97
 5 Iachino, p.166
 6 Bragadin, p.99
 7 Navy Records Society, *The Cunningham Papers Volume I* p.313
 8 Wragg, David, *Swordfish: The Story of the Taranto Raid* p.82
 9 Cunningham, A.B. *A Sailor's Odyssey* p.336
10 Ibid p.333
11 Oman, Carola, *Nelson* p.389
12 Pack, S.W.C. *Cunningham: The Commander* p.285
13 Seth, Ronald, *Two Fleets Surprised: The Battle of Matapan*, Introduction
14 Navy Records Society, *The Cunningham Papers Volume I* p.244
15 Ibid p.250
16 Playfair, Major-General I.S.O. *The Mediterranean and Middle East Volume II* p.118–119
17 Cunningham, p.363
18 MacDonald, Callum, *The Lost Battle: Crete 1941* p.134–135
19 Ibid p.300
20 Cunningham, p.379
21 Hinsley F.H. *British Intelligence in the Second World War Volume I* p.421
22 MacDonald, p.300
23 *Daily Telegraph* 28/5/1991

20

Intelligence

Almost as soon as the Italian fleet returned to its home bases after Matapan, questions began to be asked about how the British had seemed to know their every move. According to Commander Bragadin in the official history,

> Reviewing the events of the last part of March also gave rise to a suspicion that perhaps Italian plans were known to the enemy. As a matter of fact, after the war, and through documents published by the British, it was confirmed that they 'expected' an Italian move against the supply route to Crete. Beyond this, it appeared very probable that they knew that the Italian fleet had begun the above-described operation, or at least they knew the date which had been set, even before the Sunderland [flying boat] had sighted the 3rd Division.[1]

Bragadin wrote his history in 1957 long before Ultra had been declassified, but he is perceptive in his conclusions, for the British were simply too good in their movements for it to have been a matter of chance.

> All these preparations, so precise and definite, give a very firm basis for the belief that Cunningham had some specific information at hand, and that it came to him through espionage channels or through his signal intelligence service.[2]

However he notes the disastrous outcome of the night battle 'resulted from completely accidental circumstances on the part of both adversaries.'[3] Again Bragadin's perception is quite accurate:

In the Italian navy preliminary orders regarding ships and convoys were never sent by radio ... This cannot be said, however, for the ciphers of the Italian Air Force, and particularly not for those of the Luftwaffe, which were notoriously easy to decipher.

The Regia Marina could not avoid from time to time warning Superaereo (air force command) and X Cat of operations; he rightly felt that here was the weak link in the Italian chain of communications. Also in general terms it was impossible to keep complex naval operations entirely secret.

For example, the details concerning a convoy had to be communicated by Supermarina to dozens of naval, air, and army authorities, not only Italian but also German in advance of the operation. Furthermore, this work had to be done through six different and dissimilar communications and information networks.[4]

The Germans always assumed the security break must lie with their Italian allies and they had betrayed their own fleet. The code breaker Mavis Batey commented on this:

The Germans had always accused the Italians of having traitors in their midst, which was made worse when, in 1966, H. Montgomery Hyde published the story of the beautiful spy, Cynthia, who had seduced Admiral Lais, the naval attaché in the Italian Embassy in Washington, and obtained the codebook from him which resulted in the Italian defeat at Matapan.[5]

Hyde's book was a biography of the British spy Amy Elizabeth Thorpe Pack Brousse, codenamed Cynthia. Betty Pack, as she was known, was a beautiful American married to a British diplomat. She was recruited by British Intelligence in 1938 and was able to move in the aristocratic world of international diplomatic society. 'Cynthia' left war-torn Madrid during the Spanish Civil War, to besieged Warsaw and occupied Paris and later Washington. She certainly had an effect in uncovering enemy secrets; however she had little to do with Matapan.[6]

As one reviewer observed, 'treason in bed and death at sea made a libretto which sold well' and the Admiral's [Lais's] family felt obliged to take out a libel action, such a course being permitted in Italy on behalf of the dead. Montgomery Hyde was found guilty but the real evidence was not available.

However there was a glaring mistake about Matapan in Hyde's book, as its states that when Lais told Cynthia where to find the codebook, the lovers were bidding each other farewell on the ship that was to take Lais back to Italy. That departure recorded in the *New York Times* took place on 26 April 1941, almost a month after Cunningham was supposed to have used Lais's codebooks at Matapan. Also the Admiral's son was serving in the Mediterranean and it was unlikely he would ever have given up codebooks, and indeed it is extremely doubtful he had access to the Italian fleet's codebooks in the US anyway.[7]

When Ultra was declassified in 1974 and its secrets published in Winterbotham's book, *The Ultra Secret,* it exonerated the Italians and put the Germans in the frame as the culprits. However in 1978 when the records were released there was evidence that it was decoded Italian messages that gave the game away, albeit the Luftwaffe pointed the direction in which to look. The Cynthia story has been rehashed in various books continuing the myth of codebooks obtained by seduction.

According to Mavis Batey:

> I was able to scupper the idea that we had been given codebooks captured by Cynthia or anybody else, if we had such books we shouldn't have needed codebreakers as it would have been child's play ... At last the Italians had got what they needed to exonerate poor Admiral Lais. They asked me if they brought the actual Matapan battle messages from Rome whether I would show them how they had been broken individually without a code book.

A tall order for Mavis after 40 years.

Dr Giulio Divita went with the Admiral in charge of Italian naval history to see the Ultra decodes.

> When I held the message headed SUPERMARINA in my hand it seemed as if time had stood still and I was nineteen again and wearing a green jumper ... Cynthia was finally put to bed too, no seduction and no codebooks but just hard cryptographic slogging and a lucky break.[8]

Of course Admiral Cunningham knew all about this years before. Mavis met the Admiral, the 'Nelson of the Mediterranean', at Bletchley Park.

> Almost as soon as the last shot was fired, Admiral John Godfrey, the Director of Naval Intelligence, rang through to Bletchley Park with the message 'Tell Dilly that we have won a great victory in the Mediterranean and it is entirely due to him and his girls.' Our sense of elation knew no bounds when Cunningham came down in person to congratulate us a few weeks later. Somebody rushed down to the Eight Bells public house to get a couple of bottles of wine, and if it was not up to the standard of the C-in-C Mediterranean was used to, he didn't show it when he toasted 'Dilly and his girls.' 'Dilly' was Dillwyn Knox, a classical scholar, papyrologist and brilliant cryptographer from the First World War and I was one of his 'girls'.[9]

For 30 years after the war Mavis said nothing about her work at Bletchley, until the secret was finally revealed in 1974. 'I said, "This is what I did in the war." My husband said. "That's interesting. What's for tea?"'[10]

Notes

1 Bragadin, M.A. *The Italian Navy in World War II* p.99
2 Ibid p.99
3 Ibid p.100
4 Ibid p.101–103
5 Erskine Ralph & Michael Smith, *Action this Day* p.107
6 Hyde, H. Montgomery, *Cynthia. The Spy who Changed the Course of the War*
7 Sebag–Montefiore, Hugh, *Enigma: The Battle for the Code* p.130–131
8 Erskine & Smith, p.107–109
9 Ibid p.96
10 *The Times*, 7/9/2009

21

What If

What if there had been no battle of Matapan? After all the Italian fleet had been goaded into action in March 1941, mainly at the behest of their German ally; the operation seemed doomed to failure from the beginning.

Admiral Iachino was ordered to 'carry out an attack on enemy shipping in the zone south of Gavdos and in the west Aegean', to cut the British military aid to Greece from Egypt, yet the Germans did not attack Greece until 6 April. Really the Italian fleet stood little chance of achieving anything under such circumstances other than meeting the Mediterranean Fleet; far better if it had been deployed during the British retreat and evacuation from Greece and/or Crete.

On 21 April General Wavell, after meeting the Greek leaders, decided he had no alternative but immediately to embark such part of his force as he could. The attempt to try and hold Greece in the face of the German invasion had been a disaster, one long series of retreats. The withdrawal tasked Admiral Cunningham with a hazardous and intricate operation at a time when his forces were already severely taxed.[1] Operation *Demon*, as it was known, was commanded by Vice-Admiral Pridham-Wippell, with all the available cruisers and destroyers. He had his headquarters at Suda Bay, Crete, while Cunningham remained in Alexandria.

The C-in-C's policy for the evacuation was that as many men as possible were to be got away, carrying their small arms and valuable equipment such as gun sights and optical instruments. Supplies and stores of value were to be given to the Greek people; everything else would be destroyed.

Embarkation took place at widely scattered beaches. Ships laden with troops would go to Alexandria, except the landing ships *Glenearn* and *Glengyle* and the destroyers which would ply between Greece and Crete.[2]

Admiral Cunningham wrote of the operation, in which 50,672 soldiers were carried away from Greece.

> The large convoys taking the troops on from Crete to Alexandria came through without loss, and it has to be remembered that the whole operation was carried out without any cover from the battle-fleet. Every available destroyer was engaged in the actual evacuation, and none was left to take the battle-fleet to sea until the very end, when it was essential to provide cover for the large convoys to Egypt. We owed much to the inertness of the Italian fleet. Had they chosen to interfere, Operation *Demon* would have been greatly slowed up. At the worst, it might have been interrupted altogether.[3]

As it was, although Cunningham greatly regretted it, only 8,000 soldiers were left behind and forced to surrender.

Why then did the Italian fleet not put in an appearance at this critical time when it might have been effective? Also why did they not put in an appearance during the 'Tiger' convoy run from Gibraltar via Malta to Alexandria? This convoy passed through the straits of Gibraltar during the night of 5/6 May; or they could have attacked the slow convoy that left Alexandria for Malta on 5 May.

Commander Bragadin in the official Italian naval history felt an attack during the evacuation of British troops from Greece

> ... could have produced excellent results. Nevertheless, such an attack was never carried out, and there are those who criticise the navy for being as prudent in this case as it had been imprudent at the battle of Matapan.
>
> This criticism however, is only valid in retrospect. The fact the British Air Force in the eastern Mediterranean was then in a critical situation was only discovered by the Italians later. As for the British air forces at Malta, they were up to strength. Add to this the fact that the operation with only light units did not signify anything, for the Alexandria fleet was on the alert and ready to bar the way to any opposition.[4]

This seems at first glance to appear to be a catalogue of excuses. Surely moving into the Aegean north of Crete would not have been that difficult. Of course most heavy units of the Regia Marina had been moved to the northwest coast of Italy. But they should have been able to pass Malta at night, and two *Cesare* class battleships were at Taranto. However there were other considerations.

> In the Aegean the navy's ships could be protected effectively only by the 4th German Air Corps [IV Cat], just arrived from Germany. That organisation rejected the proposal to provide such cooperation. The writer has reason for believing that IV Cat did not want any Italian naval assistance in the Aegean, for it wished to keep for itself full credit for any and every victory.

Such was the relationship between the Axis allies. Also Mussolini and Supermarina had ordered the Regia Marina not to operate heavy units beyond the range of fighter cover. A similar, if not even better opportunity presented itself during the battle for Crete.

> Although several occasions that could have been exploited presented themselves, the means was lacking to take advantage of them. Beyond the reasons similar to those noted above, the decisive argument for the Italians not taking part in the campaign was IV Cat's definite affirmation that 'its planes were all that were necessary', and its ruling out of any possibility of giving the necessary air cover to the Italian naval units.[5]

Fliegerkorps IV pointed out that its pilots were unable to distinguish between friendly and enemy ships. Thus it was the Germans who threw away the use of one of the best weapons available to the Axis through their lack of training. Even then some smaller Italian ships did take part in the Crete operation and were attacked by the Luftwaffe. Stukas attacked the Italian destroyer *Sagittario* escorting German landing troops. Another group of five destroyers loaded with German troops were attacked by the Luftwaffe shortly after leaving Piraeus, resulting in one destroyer being badly damaged. All this in spite of IV Cat's orders not to attack naval units north of Crete smaller than cruisers.

Also the Germans revealed none of their plans to the Italians, not even included Italian Supreme Command. Bragadin believes this was due to the German thirst for glory. On the other hand they may have been influenced by the poor security of the Matapan operation that they believed had been compromised by Italian traitors.

In many ways the German plan to take Crete was as flawed as the British decision to defend the island. Admiral Cunningham wrote:

> Looking back I sometimes wonder whether the loss of the island was really such a serious matter it seemed at the time. Had we defeated the German attack and held the island the problem of its maintenance and supply would have been extraordinarily difficult.[6]

However he was to admit that German aircraft operating from Crete made the maintenance of Malta far more difficult from the eastern Mediterranean.

When Hitler's armies had taken mainland Greece they faced a stark choice: to continue with a Middle Eastern strategy or to turn against the Soviet Union. Of course the destruction of that country was the strategic and ideological project closest to Hitler's heart, so there was no choice for his advisors no matter how much they protested.

Oil was vital to Germany and Italy and supply was always a problem, yet ample oil lay close at hand, even closer when they had completed the conquest of Greece. Iraq, Iran and Saudi Arabia where the biggest oil producers and a direct route lay across the eastern Mediterranean, provided the Axis forces in the area were reinforced, part of which reinforcement should have been in the shape of the Italian fleet, supplied and used correctly.

The Germans could have used stepping stones, some already Axis territory, the Italian Dodecanese islands of the Turkish coast and Rhodes. An airborne assault against Cyprus might have made far better use of the 7th Airborne Division, in practice uselessly thrown away on Crete. Behind an airborne bridgehead in Cyprus and employing local shipping protected by German airpower, a sizeable amphibious assault force with the Italian fleet could have been built up for landings in Syria and Lebanon. Once secure in the French Levant, mobile columns could have moved against Iraq and onward. The oil wealth yielded would have solved all Hitler's difficulties in maintaining his military machine.[7]

When Germany invaded Yugoslavia and Greece in April 1941, she committed 27 divisions to the operation, seven of which were panzer divisions, a third of all such units in the German Army. The victory in Crete cost the Germans 8,000 troops, many drowned in ships sunk by the Mediterranean Fleet, and 400 aircraft. It disrupted any chance Hitler had to turn towards Syria and the oilfields, and proved disastrous to operations later in Russia when in October 1941 the German armies were caught by the Russian winter in front of Moscow. As Admiral Cunningham wrote 'Our defence of Crete, therefore, may have served its purpose in the overall pattern of the war.'[8] Indeed Matapan cast a long shadow.

What about the 'Tiger' convoy? Why did the Italian fleet not put to sea then? On 8 May the convoy had been sighted and the Mediterranean Fleet was located heading for the central basin. If heavy units of the Italian fleet had sailed on the evening of the 8th, they should have been able to join action some time on the 9th. Bragadin felt that the British would have moved away south, and the Italian ships would have been unable to follow.

> Furthermore, at that particular moment only the battleships *Cesare* and *Doria* were operational, as against three in the Alexandria fleet. Nor was it possible for the Italians to rely on effective air escort; yet it was certain that there would be air attacks, at least by the planes from the British aircraft carrier. On the whole, the risks were greater than the dubious results that could have been expected from the venture.

It does seem to have been the case that things were never quite right for the Regia Marina, that even when it had an advantage it was unwilling to take risks. They were also crippled by a lack of air reconnaissance; they had no idea the battleship *Queen Elizabeth* had joined the Mediterranean Fleet until informed by sources at Alexandria.

The Italian surface fleet did from time to time attempt operations but none really came off. They put to sea in August 1941 with the battleships *Littorio* and *Vittorio Veneto*, both repaired after British aerial torpedo strikes at Taranto and Matapan respectively, with several cruisers and destroyers. However, the British force from Gibraltar they were trying to intercept, consisting of the battleship *Nelson*, carrier *Ark Royal* and escorts which were on their way to carry out an operation against Sardinia, turned back after sighting the Italian ships. Cooperation between Axis naval forces and air forces seemed to have improved, but the cruise had consumed a large amount of fuel and Supermarina warned the Supreme

Command 'it is no longer possible to repeat such missions except and when they are absolutely necessary.'

In September another British convoy, 'Hulherd', was routed through to Malta from Gibraltar. Admiral Somerville's covering force included the battleships *Nelson*, *Rodney*, *Prince of Wales* and the carrier *Ark Royal*. The Italians hoped to send all five of their serviceable battleships to sea to counter the British; fuel shortages reduced the fleet to the two modern battleships. Admiral Iachino was still bound by the general policy that action was to be sought only if the Italian surface forces had a clear superiority, and by the directive issued after Matapan that they were to remain within range of land-based fighter aircraft.

The reports that reached the Italian C-in-C left him with doubts concerning the size and location of the British forces, and he was further handicapped by poor visibility. The opposing fleets never came within sight of each other.[9]

The battleship *Nelson* was hit on the port bow by a torpedo from an Italian aircraft resulting in the flooding of several compartments with thousands of gallons of water, and her speed was soon reduced to 15 knots. One of *Rodney's* officers described the Italians as attacking 'with great courage' considering the large target they presented, and they met with tremendous fire. 'Everywhere you could see them falling into the drink.'[10]

It was seen as another failure by Supermarina, according to Commander Bragadin:

On the whole its mission was marked with a depressing 'nothing to report' and with an enormous consumption of precious fuel, plus the collapse of the hopes of effective air-sea cooperation.

The Italian Air Force had actually sent heavy forces into the battle and had inflicted more than a little damage on the enemy. But it forgot completely about its promise of cooperation with the naval forces at sea.[11]

The battles of Sirte in December 1941, sometimes known as the battle of the convoys, were fought during the attempts by the Italians to run convoys to Libya while the British did the same with a convoy from Alexandria to Malta. A large Italian convoy was supported closely by the battleship *Duilio,* with further distant heavy support units consisting of *Littorio*, *Vittorio Veneto*, *Doria* and *Cesare*. On 14 December the British submarine *Urge* hit the *Vittorio Veneto* with two or three torpedoes causing serious damage, while the submarine *Upright* sank two merchant ships.

Three days later a British force commanded by Rear Admiral Philip Vian in the cruiser *Naiad* was described by a German aircraft as one battleship with cruisers and destroyers. In fact the battleship was a tanker. The Italian battle fleet headed towards it at their best speed of *Cesare's* 24 knots but were 250 miles away.

Another British force of cruisers and destroyers left Malta to meet Vian and take the tanker in. By this time Vian had been warned of the Italian battleships as they closed in and hoped to attack them at night. In Alexandria, Cunningham was frustrated.

> For me it was galling in the extreme. Part at least of the enemy fleet was at sea, and there was I, fretting and fuming at Alexandria, with my battleships immobilised in harbour through lack of a destroyer screen.[12]

By 17:00 Admiral Iachino's fleet had still not made contact with the British. With night fast approaching and no radar on his ships, and hamstrung by the necessity of protecting convoys, he decided against attacking, slowed his ships and began making preparations for the night.

Commander Bragadin wrote that at 17:30

> ... the *Littorio* group unexpectedly observed a heavy curtain of anti-aircraft fire over the horizon to the east, where it was already getting dark. It was the British group, which was defending itself against a violent attack by Italian and German planes.
>
> The *Littorio* group turned immediately towards the enemy and the tops of the superstructures of the British ships were sighted just as the sun was disappearing beyond the horizon. At 17:53, in the gathering dusk and in spite of the long range at 32,000 meters, the *Littorio* opened fire, and the other Italian ships joined in immediately.[13]

The British had been taken by surprise; Admiral Vian immediately had a smokescreen laid and moved away to break contact. Both sides sent in destroyers for a torpedo attack.

By 18:04 darkness had descended; the action lasted barely eleven minutes by which time Vian's force was cloaked in darkness. The Italian battle fleet moved back west to protect the convoy.

Commander Bragadin summed up the operation from the Italian side:

> The fact that the British did not have any aircraft carrier with them
> had contributed notably to the success of this Italian operation. On
> the Italian side, however, some of the failures of the air reconnais-
> sance were conspicuous. For example, the Italian attack on the British
> fleet grew out of the chance sighting at dusk. If Admiral Iachino had
> been more exactly informed as to the position of the enemy's ships, he
> could have established contact earlier.[14]

For the Royal Navy the last months of 1941 were a time of adversity
and heavy losses, even greater than those inflicted in the Battle of Crete.
The carrier *Ark Royal* of Force H was lost 25 miles from Gibraltar to a
U-boat on 14 November. *Barham*, a veteran of Matapan was sunk by
U331 on 25 November off the Libyan coast with a heavy loss of life. On
14 December the light cruiser *Galatea* was sunk by *U557*. Three days
later the cruiser *Neptune* and destroyer *Kandahar* were lost to mines near
Tripoli.

The loss of *Barham* was particularly shocking to Admiral Cunningham.

> I was sitting in my bridge cabin in the *Queen Elizabeth* having tea.
> I suddenly heard and half felt the door give three distinct rattles, and
> thought we had opened fire with our anti-aircraft guns. I went quickly
> up the one ladder to the bridge, and then I saw the *Barham*, immedi-
> ately astern of us, stopped and listing heavily over to port. The thuds
> I heard were three torpedoes striking her. She had been torpedoed by
> a U-boat. The poor ship rolled nearly over onto her beam ends, and
> we saw the men massing on her unturned side. A minute or two later
> there came the dull rumble of a terrific explosion as one of her maga-
> zines blew up. The ship became completely hidden in a great cloud of
> yellowish-black smoke, which went wreathing and eddying high into
> the sky. When it cleared *Barham* had disappeared.[15]

Ken Gibson remembers escaping the ERA (Engine Room Artificers)
mess on *Barham,* making his way on deck.

> I went aft, to an open water-tight door which led to ladders going
> up through the structure immediately behind 'B' turret. Climbing

ladders became increasingly difficult as the list continued. The ship was at about 30° as I struggled to get out of the upper door. I vaguely remember crawling and jumping and trying to keep my balance, before I eventually dived off the side of 'B' turret. On surfacing everything was pitch black. The ship had exploded while I was submerged. Gradually the black smoke cleared revealing a widely spread slick of bunker oil. The silence was uncanny. The only sign of movement was black heads bobbing amongst the oil covered debris.

Ronald Dando, an engine room rating, was on deck enjoying a smoke amidships leaning over the port rail when the torpedoes struck.

Men came scrambling on to the upper decks, getting from below decks as quickly as they could ... We must have been at a forty-five degree angle now with water lapping over the port side.
   It was useless jumping off the port side, there being the danger of being sucked back into the ship by water that was rushing in.

Ronald dragged himself over to the starboard side which was getting higher as the ship rolled; there he slid down the side and into the sea.

I must have been a few hundred yards astern of *Barham* when there was a terrific roar and she blew sky high, men, guns, all sorts flying through the air, a great wave. It seemed like a mile high, came rushing towards us, struggling and floundering in the swell. I remember thinking to myself, this is the end, and then the wave crashed down on us. I felt myself rammed down then whirled round and round like a cork.

Ronald was picked up by an Australian destroyer just in time.

I was getting very tired, I went down twice ... I fought my way back to the surface, the destroyers seemed miles away. I tried to float, swallowed more water and oil, I floundered helplessly just about giving up the struggle when someone put an arm around me and a voice said, 'Take it easy mate, have a breather.'

His new friend helped him to some debris where two other men were clinging from which they were all picked up.[16] There were 450 survivors, including Vice-Admiral Pridham-Wippell, from *Barham*, out of a complement of 1,311 men.

Meanwhile another crushing blow was struck, although not with such great loss of life. As Admiral Cunningham put it, something 'unpleasant' happened at Alexandria, while commander Bragadin felt 'the stars had unexpectedly favoured the Italian Navy.'

The Italians were past masters at the use of human torpedoes, the *Mignatta*, which they had used in the First World War to sink the Austrian battleship *Viribus Unitis*. The Second World War version, the two-man torpedo, was used by the Italian assault teams against British ships in Alexandria and Gibraltar. These units were organised under the Special 10th Mas Flotilla.

The 'pigs' – as the two-man torpedoes were known – were transported close to the target by conventional submarines, from which they were launched. In October 1940 they almost managed to blow up *Barham* in Gibraltar harbour but all three pigs sank because of defects. In May 1941 they tried again at Gibraltar but failed again due to breakdowns. However in September, despite new British defences against such attacks, 10th Mas managed to sink the merchant ship *Durham*, a 10,893-ton vessel loaded with ammunition, and the 8,000-ton tanker *Denbydale*.

On the night of 19 December an attack was launched against Alexandria. Commander Bragadin takes up the story, when the submarine *Scine* had worked her way skilfully within a mile of the entrance to Alexandria, on the evening of 18 December.

> There, in the immediate vicinity of a mine field three 'Pigs' were disgorged at 20:47, and the submarine turned back for home. The three torpedoes were manned by crews captained by Lieutenant Durand de la Penne, who had made the first attempt against Gibraltar, naval Engineer Captain Marceglia … and naval Ordnance Captain Martellotta. [Officers in the technical branches of the Italian Navy carried army titles of rank.]

The three torpedoes reached the port by following British destroyers through the open harbour gate. The three 'pigs' made their way to their respective targets, de la Penne *Valiant*, Marceglia the *Queen Elizabeth* and Martellotta, a large tanker.

Each crew quickly located its own target and attached the warhead of its torpedo at a predesignated point, determined by a study of the plans of the ship … de la Penne was the only one who encountered any trouble. His 'pig' stopped dead in the water a short distance from *Valiant*, but he and his companion by a tremendous effort, dragged the torpedo along the sea bottom until they were under the hull. Escaping, the two men surfaced near a buoy, where they were discovered by a patrolling motor boat.[17]

Admiral Cunningham observed what happened next.

> At about 4 am on December 19 I was called in my cabin on board the *Queen Elizabeth* with the news that two Italians had been found cling-ing to the bow buoy of the *Valiant*. They had been taken on board and interrogated; but had vouchsafed nothing and had been sent ashore under arrest.
>
> I at once ordered them bought back to the *Valiant* and confined in one of the forward compartments well below the waterline. The boats of all ships were called away to drop small charges around them, while the ships companies were turned out of their hammocks below and chain bottom lines were dragged along the ships' bottoms.[18]

Around 06:00 there was an explosion under the stern of the tanker *Sagona*, close to the *Queen Elizabeth*. The destroyer *Jervis* was alongside the tanker. Both ships were badly damaged. Repairs to the *Jervis* would take a month.

About 20 minutes later *Valiant* was blown up, and a few minutes later *Queen Elizabeth*. Cunningham was right aft by the ensign staff.

> I felt a dull thud and was tossed about five feet into the air by the whip of the ship and was lucky not to come down sprawling. I saw a great cloud of black shoot up the funnel and from immediately in front of it, and knew at once that the ship was badly damaged. The *Valiant* was already down by the bows. The *Queen Elizabeth* took a heavy list to starboard.[19]

In one blow the Italians with their 'pigs' – known to the British as 'Sea Chariots' – had changed the balance of power at sea. Two weeks earlier Japan had entered the war and crippled the US Pacific Fleet at Pearl

Harbor; three days later Japanese naval aircraft sank the British battle-ships *Prince of Wales* and *Repulse* off Malaya.

Cunningham now had only a handful of cruisers and destroyers in the Mediterranean and no carrier. *Formidable* had joined *Illustrious* in the US for repairs, the former having been badly damaged during the Battle of Crete, while the new carrier *Indomitable* had run aground. The battleship *Warspite,* Cunningham's flagship at Matapan had also been badly damaged off Crete and made her way to the west coast of the US for repairs, reaching Puget Sound Navy Yard near Seattle on 11 August.

Roger J. Paquette was working on a warship in Puget Sound that day.

We were on the quarterdeck that morning and we watched HMS *Warspite* slowly come into Port Orchard Bay to the navy yard in Sinclair Inlet. It was 8am and we heard their call to colours. We were impressed by the marines on deck formally marching with their beautiful hesitation steps [slow march] a much classier ceremony than the *Arizona*'s with its squawking public address system.[20]

Fortunately the two battleships in Alexandria harbour had settled vertically in shallow water, and all the crews of the 'pigs' were captured. These men became legends in both navies. After the war Captain C.E. Morgan of *Valiant,* by then Admiral Morgan, was chief of the Allied Naval Mission in Italy, and requested the privilege of personally pinning the Gold Medal of Honour on Durand de la Penne himself.

The British organised their own two-man diver swimmer teams with 'pigs' along Italian lines. In January 1943 at Palermo they sank the cruiser *Traiano.*

Cunningham managed to bluff out his situation in Alexandria harbour and it was weeks before the enemy realised what had happened. Rear Admiral W.J. Yendell wrote

... as I was arriving at the office I thought the *Queen Elizabeth* was lower in the water with a slight list. But for colours that day ABC had the press down; and photographs of colours and ABC were in the papers next day (with no sign of the list or the submarine alongside providing power to the stricken ship) and I believe it was months before the Italians knew the results of the attack.[21]

Valiant was lightened as much as possible and put into the floating dock. Her damage was bad, 80 feet long including the keel. It took two months to complete temporary repairs making her ready for sea.

Yet the year 1942 would prove the turning point of the war with the Allied victories at Midway, El Alamein and Stalingrad. Winston Churchill said 'Before Alamein we never had a victory. After Alamein we never had a defeat.' What about Taranto and Matapan when the Royal Navy held the ring in the Mediterranean?

The veteran battleships of Matapan, *Warspite* and *Valiant* would be back in the Mediterranean in 1943 for Operation *Husky*, the invasion of Sicily.

Notes
1 Playfair, Major-General I.S.O. *The Mediterranean and Middle East Volume II* p.95–96
2 Ibid p97
3 Cunningham, A.B. *A Sailor's Odyssey* p.356
4 Bragadin, M.A. *The Italian Navy in World War II* p.105
5 Ibid p.105–106
6 Cunningham, p.391
7 Cowley, Robert, *What If: John Keegan, How Hitler Could Have Won the War* p.301–302
8 Cunningham, p.392
9 Playfair, p.276–277
10 Ballantyne, Iain, *Rodney* p.158
11 Bragadin, p.122–123
12 Cunningham, p.431
13 Bragadin, p.148
14 Ibid p.150
15 Cunningham, p.424
16 Barham Association. www.hmsbarham.com
17 Bragadin, p.284–285
18 Cunningham, p.433
19 Ibid p.433
20 Plevy, Harry, *Battleship Sailors* p.193
21 Pack, S.W.C. *Cunningham: The Commander* p.199

Appendix A

The British Fleet at Matapan

Battleships

Warspite
Flagship of Admiral Sir Andrew Cunningham KCB DSO C-in-C
Mediterranean Fleet
Captain D.B. Fisher, CBE
30,600 tons
24 knots
8 x 15-inch
20 x 4.5-inch
She was completed at Portsmouth in 1913, then reconstructed and modernised in the 1930s. She was damaged during the battle for Crete and wrecked at Prussia Cove, Cornwall, 1947.

Valiant
Captain C.E. Morgan, DSO
32,700 tons
24 knots
8 x 15-inch
20 x 4.5-inch
She was completed at Fairfield in 1914, then reconstructed and modernised at the outbreak of war. She was sunk in Alexandria harbour in 1941 by an Italian two-man submarine, and then refloated. She was scrapped in 1948.

Barham
Flagship of 1st Battle Squadron, Rear Admiral H.B. Rawlings OBE
Captain G.C. Cooke
31,000 tons
22 knots
8 x 15-inch
12 x 6-inch
She was completed at Clydebank in 1914 and sunk in November 1941
by U331, with the loss of 861 officers and men.

Aircraft Carrier

Formidable
Flagship of Rear Admiral, Air, D.W. Boyd CBE DSC
Captain A.W. La T. Bisset
23,000 tons
30 knots
16 x 4.5-inch
She was completed at Belfast 1940. She was badly damaged during
the battle for Crete and scrapped at Inverkeithing in 1953. The aircraft squadrons embarked in *Formidable* were 803, 826, 829 (operating
from Crete: 815).

Cruisers

Orion
Flagship of Vice Admiral Light Forces Vice-Admiral H.D. Pridham-
Wippell CB CVO
Captain G.R.B. Back
7,215 tons
32 knots
8 x 6-inch
She was completed in Devonport in 1932 and scrapped in 1949.

Ajax
Captain E.D.B. McCarthy
6,985 tons
32 knots
8 x 6-inch
She was completed at Barrow in 1934 and scrapped in 1949.

Perth
RAN Captain Sir P.W. Bowyer-Smith Bart
7,165 tons
32 knots
8 x 6-inch
She was completed at Portsmouth in 1934. She was transferred to RAN in 1940 and sunk at the Battle of the Java Sea in 1942.

Gloucester
Captain H.A. Rowley
9,600 tons
32 knots
12 x 6-inch
She was completed at Devonport dockyard in 1937 and sunk by German aircraft at Crete in 1941.

Destroyers

14th Destroyer Flotilla
Jervis
Captain D.P.J. Mack DSO
1,760 tons
36 knots
6 x 4.7-inch

Janus
1,760 tons
36 knots

6 x 4.7-inch
Lost 1944

Mowhawk
1,870 tons
36 knots
8 x 4.7-inch

Nubian
1,870 tons
36 knots
8 x 4.7-inch
Badly damaged, Crete 1941

10th Destroyer Flotilla
Stuart
RAN Captain D.H.M.L. Walker DSO
1,530 tons
36 knots
4 x 4.7-inch

Greyhound
1,335 tons
36 knots
4 x 4.7-inch
Sunk at Crete 1941

Griffin
1,335 tons
36 knots
4 x 4.7-inch
Transferred to RCN 1942

2nd Destroyer Flotilla
Ilex
1,370 tons
36 knots
4 x 4.7-inch

Hasty
1,340 tons
36 knots
4 x 4.7-inch
Lost 1942

Hereward
1,340 tons
36 knots
4 x 4.7-inch
Sunk at Crete 1941

Havock
1,340 tons
36 knots
4 x 4.7-inch
Lost 1942

Hotspur
1,340 tons
36 knots
4 x 4.7-inch

Appendix B

The Italian Fleet at Matapan

Battleship

Vittorio Veneto, His Excellency Admiral Angelo Iachino's flagship.
Completed at Trieste, 1940, damaged at Matapan by an ariel torpedo,
and eight months later by torpedoes from the submarine HMS *Urge*.
After Italy surrendered, *Vittorio Veneto* was sent to the Suez Canal as war
reparations. She was scrapped in 1948.
35,000 tons
30 knots
9 x 15-inch
12 x 6-inch

Cruisers

1st Division   *Vice Admiral C. Cattaneo on Zara*
Zara
10,000 tons
32 knots
8 x 8-inch
sunk during Matapan

Fiume
10,000 tons

32 knots
8 x 8-inch
sunk during Matapan

Pola
10,000 tons
32 knots
8 x 8-inch
sunk during Matapan

3rd Division   *Vice Admiral L. Sansonetti on Trieste*
Trieste
10,000 tons
35 knots
8 x 8-inch
sunk at Sardinia by USAF bombers 1943

Trento
10,000 tons
35 knots
8 x 8-inch
sunk in the Ionian Sea by British submarine HMS *Umbra* 1942

Bolzano
10,000 tons
36 knots
8 x 8-inch
scrapped 1947

8th Division   *Vice Admiral A. Legnani on Abruzzi*
Abruzzi
7,874 tons
35 knots
10 x 6-inch
scrapped 1972

Garibaldi
7,874 tons
35 knots
10 x 6-inch
scrapped 1976

Destroyers

6th Destroyer Flotilla
Da Recco
1,628 tons
39 knots
6 x 4.7-inch

Pessagno
1,628 tons
39 knots
6 x 4.7-inch
sunk by the British submarine HMS *Turbulent* 1942

9th Destroyer Flotilla
Gioberti
1,568 tons
39 knots
4 x 4.7-inch
sunk by the British submarine HMS *Simoom* 1943

Alfieri
1,568 tons
39 knots
4 x 4.7-inch
sunk during Matapan

Carducci
1,568 tons
39 knots
4 x 4.7-inch
sunk during Matapan

10th Destroyer Flotilla
Maestrale
1,449 tons
39 knots
4 x 4.7-inch
scuttled 1943

Libeccio
1,449 tons
39 knots
4 x 4.7-inch
sunk by the British submarine HMS *Upholder*, 1941

Scirocco
1,449 tons
39 knots
4 x 4.7-inch
sunk in a storm, 1942

Grecale
1,449 tons
39 knots
4 x 4.7-inch

12th Destroyer Flotilla
Corazziere
1,620 tons
39 knots
5 x 4.7-inch
scuttled 1943

Carabiniere
1,620 tons
39 knots
5 x 4.7-inch

Ascari
1,620 tons
39 knots
5 x 4.7-inch
sunk by a mine 1942

13th Destroyer Flotilla
Granatiere
1,620 tons
39 knots
5 x 4.7-inch
sunk Palermo harbour 1943

Fucillere
1,620 tons
39 knots
5 x 4.7-inch
sunk by USAF bombers, La Spezia 1943

Bersagliere
1,620 tons
39 knots
5 x 4.7-inch

Alpino
1,620 tons
39 knots
5 x 4.7-inch

Appendix C

The Aircraft at Matapan

Type	Armament	crew	cruising speed	max speed	range	service
Fulmar/ Fighter	8x.303	2	150	200	722	FAA
Albacore/ Multi/R	2x.303	3	100	144	850	FAA
Swordfish/ Multi/R	2x.303	2	90	120	465	FAA
Blenheim/ Fighter/B	2x.303	3	145	234	810	RAF
C.R.42/ Recon	2x12.7mm	1	132	238	470	RA
S 79/ Bomber	3x12.7, 2x7.7mm	5	137	224	1,050	RA
JU 88/ Fighter/B	7x7.9mm	4	171	260	1,150	Luftwaffe

Bibliography

Andrew, Christopher *Secret Service* (Heinemann, 1985)

Arthur, Max *The True Glory: The Royal Navy* (Hodder & Stoughton, 1996)

—— *Lost Voices of the Royal Navy* (Hodder & Stoughton, 1997)

Ballantyne, Iain *HMS Warspite* (Pen & Sword, 2001)

—— HMS *Rodney* (Pen & Sword, 2008)

De Belot, R. *The Struggle for the Mediterranean 1939–1945* (Princeton University Press, 1951)

Bosworth, R.J.B. *Mussolini* (Hodder Headline, 2002)

Bradford, Ernle *The Mediterranean: Portrait of a Sea* (Penguin, 2000)

Bragadin, M.A. *The Italian Navy in World War II* United States Naval Institute Annapolis Maryland, 1957)

Buckley, Christopher *Greece and Crete 1941* (HMSO, 1952)

Bullock, Alan *Hitler: A Study in Tyranny* (Odhams Press, 1954)

Causley, Charles *Hands to Dance and Skylark* (Antony Mott, 1951)

Ciano, Count Galeazzo *Ciano's Diary 1937–1943* (Methuen & Co, 1952)

Cooper, Artemis *Cairo in the War 1939–1945* Hamish Hamilton 1989)

Connell, John *Wavell Supreme Commander* (Collins, 1969)

Coward, Commander R.B. *Battleship at War* (Ian Allan, 1987)

Cowley, Robert *What If: How Hitler Could Have Won the War* (Macmillan, 2000)

Cunningham, A.B. *A Sailor's Odyssey* (Hutchinson, 1951)

Deakin, F.W. *The Brutal Friendship* (Weidenfeld & Nicolson, 1962)

Denham H.M. *The Aegean* (John Murray, 1963)

Elliott, Peter *The Cross and the Ensign: A Naval History of Malta* (Harper Collins, 1994)

Eppler, John *Operation Condor: Rommel's Spy* (MacDonald & Jane's, 1974)

Erskine Ralph & Michael Smith *Action this Day* (Bantam Press, 2001)

Farrugia, Mario *Fort Rinella* (Heritage Books, 2004)

Frankland Nobel & Christopher Dowling (eds) *Decisive Battles of the Twentieth Century* (Sedgwick & Jackson, 1976)

Garibaldi, Luciano *Mussolini: The Secrets of his Death* (Enigma Books, 2004)

Hinsley F.H. *The British Intelligence in the Second World War* (HMSO, 1979)

Hore, Captain Peter *The Habit of Victory* (Sidgwick & Jackson, 2005)

Hyde, H. Montgomery *Cynthia: The Spy who Changed the Course of the War* (Hamish Hamilton, 1966)

Iachino, Admiral Angelo *Gaudo & Matapan* (Arnoldo Mondadori, 1946)

Kesselring A. *The Memories of Field Marshal Kesselring* (Greenhill Books, 1988)

Lamb, Charles *War in a Stringbag* (Cassell, 1977)

Lewin, Ronald *Rommel as Military Commander* (Barnes & Noble, 1998)

MacDonald, Callum *The Lost Battle: Crete 1941* (Macmillan, 1993)

Montagu, Ewen *Beyond Top Secret Ultra* (Coward, McCann, & Geoghegan, 1978)

Morgan, Philip *The Fall of Mussolini* (Oxford University Press 2007)

Navy Records Society *The Cunningham Papers Volume 1: The Mediterranean Fleet 1939–1942* (Ashgate, 1999)

Oman, Carola *Nelson* (Hodder & Stoughton, 1947)

Pack, S.W.C. *The Battle of Matapan* (B.T. Batsford, 1961)

—— *Cunningham: The Commander* (B.T. Batsford, 1974)

—— *The Battle for Crete* (Ian Allan, 1973)

Perowne, Stewart *The Siege Within the Walls* (Hodder & Stoughton, 1970)

Pike, Richard *Seven Seas, Nine Lives: A Biography of Captain A. W.F. Sutton* (Pen & Sword, 2006)

Pitt, Barrie *The Crucible of War: Wavell's Command* (Jonathan Cape, 1980)

Playfair, Major-General I.S.O. *The Mediterranean & Middle East Volume I* (HMSO, 1954)

—— *The Mediterranean & Middle East Volume II* (HMSO, 1956)

Plevy, Harry *Battleship Sailors* (Chatham Publishing, 2001)

Poolman, Kenneth *Experiences of War: The British Sailor* (Arms and Armour Press, 1989)

Preston, Antony *Jane's Fighting Ships of World War II* (Random House, 2001)

Schom, Alan *Trafalgar: Countdown to Battle 1803–1805* (Michael Joseph, 1990)

Sebag-Montefiore, Hugh *Enigma: The Battle for the Code* (Weidenfeld & Nicolson, 2000)

Seth, Ronald *Two Fleets Surprised: The Story of the Battle of Cape Matapan* (Geoffrey Bles, 1960)

Smith, Peter C. *Hit First, Hit Hard. HMS Renown 1916–1948* (William Kimber, 1979)

Tedder A. W. *With Prejudice: The War Memoirs of Marshal of the Royal Air Force, Lord Tedder* (Little Brown, 1966)

Van Der Vat, Dan *Standard of Power* (Pimlico, 2001)

Warner, Oliver *Cunningham of Hyndhope* (John Murray, 1967)

West, Nigel *GCHQ: The Secret Wireless War 1900–1986* (Weidenfeld & Nicolson, 1986)

Wragg, David *Swordfish: The Story of the Taranto Raid* (Weidenfeld & Nicolson, 2003)

Sources

Archives

Fleet Air Arm Museum

Imperial War Museum

Italian Navy Historical Archives

Public Records Office, Kew

Royal Navy Museum, Portsmouth

United States Navy Historical Center

Journals and Newspapers

Daily Telegraph

Sunday Telegraph

Military History Magazine

New York Times

The Times

International Fleet Review Magazine

Associations
HMS *Barham* Association
HMS *Formidable* Association
HMS *Hood* Association
HMAS *Stuart* Association

Index

Abwehr, German Intelligence Service 22, 85, 89
Aegean Sea 48, 81, 90
Afrika Korps 31, 88, 75
Albania 19, 47, 48, 55, 61
  port of Durazzo 48
  port of Valona 47
Alexandria 33–36, 47, 50, 57, 63, 65, 67–69, 77–78, 80, 84, 87, 93, 95, 97–98, 105–106, 116, 129, 135–136, 141, 155–156, 159–161
  Dekheila airfield 91
  Dekheila magazines 25
  Italian attack on 164–166
  Japanese consul 89–91
  oil storage and drydocks at 23, 27
  sailors run-ashore in 40–42
Armstrong's of Newcastle 12
Auffret Donald, signalman 122
Badoglio, Marshal Pietro 56, 61
Barnard, Commander Geoffrey 116, 122
Batey, Keith 86
Bayley, Lieutenant A. 54
Boyd, Captain Denis 47, 64–65, 98, 103
BEF 17
Benghazi 35–36, 79, 98
Blenkhorn, Petty Officer 107

Bletchley Park 29–30, 85–86, 148, 154
Bolt, Lieutenant-Commander A.S. 104, 108–109, 113–115
Bragadin, Commander Marc Antonio 20, 36, 47, 70, 75, 94, 133, 141, 156–157, 164
  on intelligence 156–157
  on Matapan 159–162
  on radar 43
  Taranto Raid 54
British Army 23–25, 84, 147
Buist, Able Seaman Christopher 83–84
Burnett, Commander Bob 88
Cagliari 35, 50
Cain, Petty Officer Bill 59
Canaris, Admiral Wilhelm 22
Cape Matapan 43, 73, 135
  Mani Peninsula 73
Cape Spartivento 58–61
Capri, Island of 80
Caruana Joseph 66
Cattaneo, Admiral Carlo 80, 95, 108, 111, 116–117, 119, 121, 124–125, 129–130, 136, 143
Causley, Charles 40
Cavagnari, Admiral Domenico 61
Cephalonia 51
Chamberlain, Neville 27, 29

Churchill, Clementine 17
Churchill, Winston 17, 23, 26, 29, 31, 34, 47, 55, 59–60, 147–150, 167
Ciano, Admiral Costanzo 15
Ciano, Count Galeazzo 15, 22, 40, 47, 55, 61, 63
Colpays, Commander Geoffrey 30
Commonwealth War Graves Commission 54
Cooke, Lieutenant 107
Copeman, Lieutenant-Commander 109
Copenhagen, battle of 145
Corsica 11, 70
  Boniface strait 70
Corsi, Captain L. 129–130
Crete 47–48, 50, 63, 77–81, 83–84, 87, 90–91, 94, 102, 105–106, 109, 111, 113–115, 117, 135, 139, 144, 146–151, 155–159, 162, 166
  Cape Krio 117
  Gavdos Island 90, 105
  Maleme 87, 91, 99, 105, 109, 113–115
  Suda Bay 48, 67, 77, 80, 83–84, 90, 104, 108, 110, 115, 135, 155
Cunningham, Admiral of the Fleet Andrew Browne 12, 20–21, 23–24, 26–27, 33, 40–43, 45, 47–49, 57, 60–65, 67–69, 81, 83, 88–90, 94–95, 103–104, 106, 109–110, 119–122, 124, 126, 130, 151, 153–156, 158–159, 161–162, 164–166
  Calabria 35–38
  conclusions 143–150
  intelligence reports 84–85
  Matapan decisions 115–116
  Matapan night action 139
  race to engage 97–100
  Taranto 51
Cyprus 149, 158
Dalyell–Stead, Lieutenant-Commander J. 105, 107
Dando, Ronald 163
Dardanelles 88

Darlan, Admiral Jean 33
Dartmouth 88
De la Penne, Lieutenant Durand 164–166
De Pisa, Captain M. 111, 129, 133
Divita, Dr Giulio 153
Dunkirk 17
Edelsten, Commodore John 121
Eisenhower, General Dwight 145
Ellis, Lieutenant 105, 110
El Alamein, battle of 167
Emmanuel III, King Victor 21
Emmington, Roy 122
Enigma Code 84, 85
Enigma Machine 29–30, 85
Eppler, John 78, 89
Favagrossa, General Carlo 16
Fisher, Captain Douglas 124
Fisher, Admiral William Wordsworth 48, 144
Fleet Air Arm 21, 46, 49, 55, 83, 86–87, 91, 106, 109, 144, 146, 150
Fleet Air Arm Squadrons
  806 47, 64, 91
  810 69
  813 51
  815 45, 51, 91, 109, 113, 144
  819 51, 53
  824 36, 51
  826 91, 99, 105, 113
  829 91, 99, 103, 113
Force H 26, 34–35, 42–43, 50, 57–58, 60, 61, 63, 65, 68–70, 78, 162
Fort Rinella 12
Freyberg General Bernard 149
Gafaar, Salah 89
Genoa 68–69
Gensoul, Admiral 34
Gibraltar 12, 23, 26, 32, 34, 42, 48, 57, 59, 63, 68, 70, 156, 159–160, 162, 164
Gibson, ERA Ken 162
Giorg, Captain G. 129, 130
Godfrey, Admiral John 30, 154
Grey, Captain A.W. 58

Guzzoni, General Alfredo 142
Haifa 24, 87
Hale, Lieutenant Commander J.W. 53
Haworth, Lieutenant Mike 105, 107
Hitler, Adolf 15, 17, 21, 48, 61, 63,
  158–159
Holland, Captain C.S 34
Hussein, Ahmed 89
Hyde, H. Montgomery 152–153
Iachino, Admiral Angelo 61, 70,
  93–95, 104–107, 114, 116–117, 119,
  129–130, 136–137, 146, 155, 160–162
  appears before Mussolini 141–144
  doubts about Operation *Gaudo*
  78–81
  engages British Fleet 98–100
  withdraws fleet 110–111
Ionian Sea 47–48, 176
Italian Special Forces 83
Jefferies, John 85
Jones, Stoker Albert 64
Keevil, Surgeon Commander 67
Kesselring, Field Marshal Albert
  76–77, 82
Knox, Dillwyn 85, 86, 154
Kreigsmarine 16
Lamb, Charles 45, 50, 53, 64, 141
Lais, Admiral Alberto 152–153
La Spezia 79, 179
Lee, Captain Hugh 84
Lee-Barber, John 97
Leros 57, 95
Lever (later Batey), Mavis 85, 152–153
Livorno (Leghorn) 20, 78
Luftwaffe 29, 63, 65–66, 70, 75, 77,
  79–81, 84, 106, 147, 152–153, 157
  Fliegerkorps X 63, 66, 75, 77–78,
  80, 84
  Fliegerkorps IV 157
  X Cat German Air Command 79,
  105, 152
Lustre Convoys 84
Lyster, Captain Lumley St George 49,
  64

MacDonald, Callum 149
MacDonnell, J.E 98
Mack, Captain Philip 110, 116, 126,
  132–133, 145
Mackintosh, Commander Lachlan 49
Majorca 69
Malta 11–12, 21, 24–26, 35–36,
  40, 42–43, 47–48, 50, 54, 57–59,
  61, 63–68, 77, 80, 87–88, 98, 135,
  156–158, 160–161
  Floriana 12
  Grand Harbour 24
  Hal Far 67
  Luqa 67
  Pieta 12
  Rinella 12
  Valetta 12
Marceglia, Captain 164
Martellotta, Captain 164
Masri, Aziz El 89
Merano 75
Morgan, Captain, C.E 166
Muslim Brotherhood 89
Mussolini, Benito 11, 15–18, 20–22,
  40, 47, 63, 85, 141–143, 157
Naples 31, 59, 63, 79, 84, 111
Navarino 36, 81
Nelson, Admiral Horatio 24, 88, 113,
  145–146, 154
New York Times 16, 153
Napoleon Bonaparte 150
Norman, Kathleen 66–67
O'Conner, General Richard 88
Oliver, Lieutenant Commander
  Geoffrey 88
Operation *Catapult* 34
Operation *Demon* 155–156
Operation *Excess* 63
Operation *Gaudo* 85, 137, 142
Operation *Husky* 167
Operation *Judgement* 45, 47, 49, 51, 53,
  55, 145
Operation *Lustre* 84, 87
Operation *Mercury* 148

Operation *Mincemeat* 31
Operation *Sea Lion* 48
Operation *Yellow* 29
Pacey, Petty Officer Maurice 104, 109
Pack, Betty (Amy Elizabeth Thorpe
    Pack Brousse) 152
Pack, Lieutenant S.W.C 91, 120, 124,
    136
Paquette, Roger, J. 166
Parodi, Sub-Lieutenant Giorgi
    129–130, 134
Pasha, Aly Maher 24
Pasha, Mohammad Mahmoud 24
Petain, Marshal Philippe 23
Piraeus 84, 90, 157
Port Said 24–25
Portsmouth 25–26
Pound, Admiral Dudley 23, 41, 48–49,
    147
Power, Captain Manley L. 89
Pridham-Wippell, Admiral H.D 55,
    90, 95, 97–99, 102, 109–110, 119–120,
    126, 145–146, 155, 164
Puget Sound Navy Yard 166
Raeder, Admiral Erich 75–76
RAF 21, 24, 26, 30, 36, 49, 54, 57, 63,
    66, 68, 90, 94, 106, 108, 147–148
RAF Squadrons
    84 90, 106, 108
    113 90, 106, 108
    211 90, 108
    228 36
    230 89, 93
    252 40
Red Sea 24, 42, 67
Regia Aeronautica 16, 20–21, 35–36,
    38, 40, 42, 48, 61, 63, 70, 76, 106, 142
Regia Marina 16, 19–21, 36, 38, 40,
    42, 47, 63, 70, 80–81, 84, 142, 152,
    157, 159,
Rejewski, Martin 29
Rhodes 77, 84, 100, 105–106, 146, 158
Riccardi, Admiral Arturo 21, 61,
    75–76, 79–80, 142

Rice, Petty Officer Pilot Ben 104,
    108–109, 115
'Ring of Iron' group 89
Rome 15, 17, 21, 40, 42, 54, 61, 76–77,
    79–80, 86–87, 105, 141, 153
    Palazzo Venezia 15–16, 142–143
    Rome Radio 40, 87
Rommel, Field Marshal Erwin 22, 31,
    78, 82, 88
Room 13 30–31
Room 39 30
Royal Navy 19, 21, 23–25, 32, 44,
    46–48, 50, 145, 149, 162, 167
    Mediterranean Fleet 41, 47, 57, 63,
    65, 77, 87–88, 93, 141, 146–147, 149,
    155, 159
Sansonetti, Admiral 81, 96–99, 116,
    131
Sansonetti, Sub-Lieutenant Vito 131
Sardinia 11, 60, 68, 70, 159
    Tirso Dam 68–69
Saunt, Lieutenant-Commander
    Gerald 100, 113–114
Scott, Commander Walter 133
Ships, British
    Ajax 43, 120
    Arethusa 25
    Ark Royal 34–35, 42, 45, 50, 57–60,
    63, 65, 68–70, 159–160, 162
    Barham 9, 26, 50, 57, 87, 91, 99, 103,
    105, 120, 131, 162–164
    Berwick 50, 57–59
    Calcutta 42
    Courageous 45
    Coventry 42 47
    Denbydale 164
    Despatch 57–58
    Devonshire 26
    Durham 164
    Fiji 147
    Formidable 65, 68, 78, 91, 94–95,
    98–100, 102–108, 110, 113–116,
    120–121, 124–125, 135–136, 146, 166
    Galatea 162

Gallant 64, 84

Glasgow 50

Glenearn 156

Glengyle 156

Glorious 26, 48–49, 144

Gloucester 35, 37, 42, 65–66, 90, 97, 99–100, 102, 120

Greyhound 120, 122, 126, 129, 132–133

Griffin 97–98, 120, 126, 132–133

Havock 120, 125–126, 131–132, 145

Hasty 90

Hereward 90

Hood 34, 88

Illustrious 42, 45–47, 49–51, 54–55, 57, 63–68, 91, 144, 146, 166

Indomitable 166

Jervis 110, 132–133, 165

Juno 115

Kandahar 162

Kent 41

Liverpool 35, 42

King George V 19

Malaya 26–27, 35, 41–42, 61, 68

Manchester 57–58

Mowhawk 110

Naiad 147, 161

Nelson 159–160

Neptune 35, 37–38, 162

Newcastle 57–58

Norfolk 26, 68

Nubian 110, 133

Orion 35, 37, 66, 90, 97, 99, 120

Pericles 83

Perth 66

Phoenix 35

Prince of Wales 160, 166

Queen Elizabeth 19, 25, 147, 159, 162, 164–166

Ramillies 57–59

Renown 42, 57–59, 62, 68–69

Repulse 166

Resolution 34, 69

Resource 24

Rodney 88, 160

Royal Sovereign 25, 35, 37, 40–41

Sagona 165

Scorpion 88

Sheffield 42 57–58 68

Southampton 57–58, 65–66

Stuart 98, 120–122, 126, 131

Suffolk 26

Sydney 35

Terror 66

Urge 161

Upright 161

Valiant 11, 34, 42, 65, 77, 91, 99–100, 103–104, 120, 124, 144, 164–167

Vendetta 90, 97

Warspite 11, 26–27, 33, 35–38, 41–42, 47, 61, 65, 90–91, 98–100, 103–104, 108–109, 113–115, 119–122, 124–125, 129–130, 135, 166–167

Ships, Italian

Abruzzi 80, 111

Alciane 43

Alfieri 124–125, 131

Alpino 114

Andrea Doria 19, 70, 159–160

Aquila 22, 143

Artigliere 43

Augustus 22, 143

Bolzano 37, 70, 81, 102, 111

Caio Duilio 12, 19, 42, 53–55. 69, 160

Carducci 125

Conte di Cavour 21, 37, 42, 53–55

Fiume 80, 111, 117, 121–122, 124–125, 129–131

Garibaldi 80, 108, 111

Gioberti 125, 136

Giulio Cesare 37, 42, 57, 63–64, 70, 157, 159–161

Gorizia 54

Gradisca 135

Grecale 126

Impero 19

Lanciere 59

Libeccio 137
Littorio (later renamed *Italia*) 11, 19, 38, 42, 53–55, 68, 99, 159–161
Maestrale 137
Oriani 125–126 137
Pola 80, 111, 114–117, 119, 121, 124, 129, 131–133, 135, 142, 144
Roma (battleship) 11, 20
Roma (merchant ship) 22, 143
Sagittario 157
Scine 164
Sparviero 22, 143
Traiano 166
Trento 70, 81, 110
Trieste 70, 81, 97, 111
Vittorio Veneto 11, 19, 38, 42, 54, 57, 59, 68, 70, 79, 80, 81, 84, 93, 94, 95, 97, 98, 99, 100, 102, 104–111, 113, 114, 115, 116, 117, 119, 120, 124, 126, 129, 132, 135, 136, 137, 143–145, 159–161
Zara 80, 108, 111, 117, 121, 124–125, 129–130, 136
Ships, French
 Bretagne 34
 Dunkerque 26, 34–35
 Strasbourg 26, 34
Ships, US
 USS *Arizona* 166
 USS *Monitor* 12
Sicily 11, 40, 53, 58, 63, 80, 105, 107, 137, 141, 167
 Augusta 40, 137
 Mount Etna 53
 Messina Straits 40, 70, 77, 79, 81
Slaughter, Lieutenant H.J. 54
Smith, Leading Steward Ted 59
Smuts, Jan 23
Somerville, Admiral 34, 58–60, 68–69, 160
Sorley, Surgeon-Commander E.R. 9, 87, 91, 136
Spanish Civil War 19, 85, 152
Spezia 11, 69, 70, 79

Stalingrad 167
Stewart, Brigadier Keith 149
Supermarina 22, 36, 42–43, 54, 57, 60, 63, 70, 77, 79–80, 85, 93–94, 105–107, 111, 116–117, 119, 129, 137, 152–153, 157, 159
Taranto 10, 12, 36, 47–50, 54–58, 68, 77, 79–80, 104, 110, 119, 137, 144–145, 150, 157, 159, 167
 San Pietro Island 53
 Cape Rondinella 53
Tedder, Air Marshal A.W. 89
Tiger Convoy 147, 156, 159
Tobruk 79, 98, 106
Torrens-Spence, Lieutenant Michael 53–54, 109, 113–115, 144
Tovey, Admiral John 33, 35–37
Trafalgar, Battle of and Day 49, 113, 136, 145
Tripoli 57, 88, 147, 162
Turing, Alan 85
U*331* 162
U*557* 162
Ultra 29–32, 85, 89, 148–151, 153
Vian, Rear Admiral Philip, later Admiral of the Fleet 89, 161
Von Milch, Field Marshal Erhard 61
Wavell, General Archibold 23, 26, 48, 147–148, 155
Watkins, Lieutenant G.R.G. 132
Welchman, Gordon 30, 85
Wilkinson, Captain B.J.H 100
Williamson, Lieutenant-Commander Kenneth 51, 54
Willougby, Commander Guy 49
Wilson, General J. 148
Wright, Chief Petty Officer Charles 69
Yendell, Admiral W.J. 166
Young Egypt 89
Zebrugge Raid 88